The Commonist Horizon: Futures beyond Capitalist Urbanization
Edited by Mary N. Taylor and Noah Brehmer

ISBN: 978-1-94217-371-7 | EBook ISBN: 978-1-94217-381-6
Library of Congress Number: 2022947571
10 9 8 7 6 5 4 3 2 1

Common Notions
c/o Interference Archive
314 7th St.
Brooklyn, NY 11215

Common Notions
c/o Making Worlds Bookstore
210 S. 45th St.
Philadelphia, PA 19104

www.commonnotions.org
info@commonnotions.org

Lost Property Press, Vilnius, Lithuania
https://lostpropertypress.com
press.lostproperty@gmail.com

LITHUANIAN
COUNCIL FOR
CULTURE

The editors acknowledge the generous support of the Lithuanian Council for Culture.

Discounted bulk quantities of our books are available for organizing, educational, or fundraising
purposes. Please contact Common Notions for more information.

Cover design by Josh MacPhee / Antumbra Design
Layout design and typesetting by Graciela "Chela" Vasquez / Chelitas Design

Printed by union labor in Canada on acid-free, recycled paper

MIX
Paper from
responsible sources
FSC
www.fsc.org   FSC® C103567

The Commonist Horizon

The Commonist Horizon
Futures beyond Capitalist Urbanization

Edited by Mary N. Taylor and Noah Brehmer

Brooklyn, NY
Philadelphia, PA
commonnotions.org

Contents

Acknowledgments

This book emerged over the course of a year in close dialogue with comrades both near and far from Vilnius. The movement space Luna6, in Vilnius, has been an integral infrastructure for this process, helping us facilitate the community gatherings, talks, discussions, and website that made this book possible. Then there are all those who contributed to our discussions as comrade thinkers and critics along the way: from Jovana Timotijević, Iva Čukić, Sonja Dragović (the Balkans); to Márton Szarvas (Hungary); on to Aleksandra Bilewicz (Poland); and Evelina Šimkutė, Tadas Šarūnas, Vilnius Social Club and Aušra Vismantaitė (Lithuania); among so many others.

Finally, a big thanks to the entire team at Common Notions who took us under their wing, helping us to achieve a miraculously quick turnaround to meet our deadlines, and partnering to launch Lost Property Press. We're grateful to Malav Kanuga for all his support with the challenges of producing a dialogical edited volume, Josh McPhee both for his cover design (that's Vilnius!) and his patient reworkings in several rounds, and Erika Biddle for invaluable editorial work and meticulous copyedits!

Preface

Stavros Stavrides

As global capitalism is becoming more and more threatening to the survival of humanity and the entire planet, the need to reconsider strategies and tactics for social emancipation and collective power becomes even more urgent. This is not an issue in which contemplation and abstract planning are adequate responses. Around the world, collectives and movements are producing valuable commoning experiences, practicing the risks and potentialities included in showing that a different future is possible. Initiatives of solidarity have flourished during the recent pandemic crisis and gesture towards radically new ways of social organization based on mutual care and equality. Networks of mutual care have united efforts even in the most difficult period of lockdowns, and sharing economies have acquired a renewed momentum, as the CareNotes Collective details in their contribution to this volume.

Do these scattered efforts, often not in touch with one another, show that the longing for a different society is buried under the exigencies of survival? Can we learn important lessons from the ways solidarity is re-invented as a necessity within organized practices of collective survival—especially by urban poor, marginalized, and dispossessed people? Is it possible to answer the questions of strategy without taking into consideration the *survival inventiveness* of the most exploited among us, and their efforts to establish alternative practices of cultural production that give shape to aspirations of emancipation?

In the context of such questions, the city and problems related to reclaiming the collective power to *create the city* become crucial. Urban populations produce knowledges, sensibilities, as well as struggles that show that a different urban future is possible. In so many places across the planet "urban extractivism," which explicitly or implicitly appropriates urban goods and services in order to convert them into real estate ventures and profit-making opportunities, needs to be confronted by local as well as interconnected global struggles.

Enclosure is the term that literally as well as metaphorically represents dominant practices of predatory dispossession. Commoning encompasses the practices that move in the opposite direction of what several authors in this edited collection refer to as *capital's spatial fix*, to reclaim what should be shared as common as well as to produce more areas of sharing. In observing struggles and initiatives that follow this path, can we discern answers to the question of collective power? Sharing power and responsibilities, participatory habits based on the rotation of duties, implementing rules based on agreements that do not suppress differences, the production of knowledge based on ideas of complementarity and synergy rather than on dogmatic approaches to eternal truths: this is the legacy of such collective experiences. Isn't this, at the same time, a genuine production of theory and politics?

This is how the questions about social organization can be reconsidered, the editors of *The Commonist Horizon* instruct us, in their collection of geographically and historically disparate commons. Distinct historical circumstances raise different issues of power distribution. The crafting of the state in neoliberal capitalism conditions is essentially a recasting of centralized power into a model that supports and serves the most powerful actors of a globalized market. In Eastern Europe and elsewhere, was state socialism a true alternative to this present we have to live in? Or is it that the most promising experiments of both the past and the future share a common effort to establish horizontality, mutual support, and equality? What can we learn from the different real-existing forms of social organization that, no matter what word used—true democracy, self-management, socialism, or anarchism—express social emancipation as a process that can only flourish in societies which consider their members as equal?

Let us hear what the contributors of this volume have to say as they chart out the commonist horizon. Their engagement in struggles for commons, and their commoning aspirations, promise a rich offering of possibilities concerning the power that commoning has to support efforts for a just society. But let us not forget, we will make the path towards this society as we walk it.

Athens, Greece
September 2022

Introduction

Noah Brehmer and Mary N. Taylor

As a microdistrict bordering the commercial core of the post-Soviet city Vilnius enters the first stages of municipality-led gentrification process, a leftist movement space—Luna6—is confronted with an urgent question: how do we move from defensive tactics that respond to the latest stages of gentrification, to transformative strategic revolts that attack its root causes and put into practice alternative forms of urban life? Today "the commons" rolls off many tongues as an answer to this question. The commons, or *commoning*, in the tradition from which we write, is a revolutionary proposal for the communal organization and control of the manifold realities that make up our daily reproduction. From cooperative housing to district kitchens, autonomous health clinics and community gardens, then scaling up to solidarity economies, we approach commoning as a horizon for reimagining and transforming social life against and beyond capitalist urbanization and accumulation.

While the commons and commoning have deep global historical roots, the approach to commoning we locate ourselves within is temporally aligned with the Midnight Notes Collective's analysis of capital's "new enclosures" in the 1990s. Pointing to the fall of the USSR, the free marketization of China, the effects of debt austerity imposed on African countries by the IMF and World Bank, and other examples of the "mutual contraction of the 'right to subsist,'" the collective finds a new phase of capital accumulation.[1] What Marx called original accumulation—the violent displacement of peoples from the means of their subsistence—is not a singular

---

1. Midnight Notes, "Introduction to the New Enclosures," *Midnight Notes* 10 (Jamaica Plain, MA: Midnight Notes, 1990).

event "at the dawn of capitalism," but rather, "a regular return to the path of accumulation and a structural component of class struggle."[2] Identifying several features of the restructuring of accumulation on a global scale since the 1970s, the goal of which was "to uproot workers from the terrain on which their organizational power is built," Midnight Notes argued that "every struggle against enclosure and for the commons becomes a call of jubilee." Their project reinvigorated the language of the commons and produced a long and ongoing study of practices and relations of commoning.[3]

Combating the new enclosures that have been advancing a planetary assault on our day-to-day existence, commoning has become a way to describe and inspire new forms of global rebellions against capital. Connecting the urban and rural, the waged and unwaged, commoning movements arise in many forms, in response to the dismantling of the social infrastructures of welfare and socialist states and the expropriation of peoples from their land and homes through privatization, enclosure, debt, and predatory financialization processes. Although at times catalyzed as a response to these global movements of enclosure, commoning is more than an appeal to the state as the guardian of the public good. The commons/commoning affirms the direct control of institutions and resources by the communities that produce and depend on them.

Much thinking about commoning has been inspired by Latin American movements—for example, the Zapatistas in Mexico (who famously rose up against NAFTA, fashioned our critiques of neoliberalism, and self-govern an autonomous territory in Chiapas today), and the protagonists of the Water War in Cochabamba, Bolivia, la Coordinadora de Defensa del Agua y de la Vida, who successfully fought against a multinational corporation's privatization of both public waterworks and self-built water supply systems. There are also long traditions in Eastern Europe—for example, the "everyday communism" of the cooperativist movement in early twentieth-century Poland—that have been taken up by some contemporary theorists as "a prefiguration of today's politics of the common." Many non-state-centric socialisms, anarchisms, and manners of commoning are part of the history of the region.[4] Histories of Czechoslovakian councilism, the

---

2. Midnight Notes, "The New Enclosures," 1.

3. Midnight Notes, "The New Enclosures," 3 and 9.

4. See Cezary Rudnicki, "An Ethics for Stateless Socialism: An Introduction to Edward Abramowski's Political Philosophy," *Praktyka Teoretyczna* 1, no. 27 (2018); Bartłomiej Błesznowski and Mikołaj Ratajczak, "Principles of the Common: Towards a Political Philosophy of Polish Cooperativism," *Praktyka Teoretyczna* 1, no. 27 (2018): 98–124.

communal subsistence economies across the Soviet Union, and experiments with self-management in Yugoslavia have much to contribute to contemporary commoning movements. By centering cities in Eastern Europe in three chapters in this book, we contribute to knowledge about traditions in this region that led to state socialist experiments, critiqued them, or fell outside their purview.

As the state socialism that came to dominate Eastern Europe (albeit with some variety) crumbled in crises of debt and legitimacy, experiments with market socialism gave way to full-on shock therapy induced neoliberalism. Activists in the region have taken up practices of commoning and ideas of the commons to criticize and counter the vicious wave of enclosures that became apparent after the fall of state socialism, without seeking a return to its heavily stigmatized politics and policies. The commons have also been embraced within some of these same movement formations to think about the many practices and struggles that appeared under and within existing state socialism, beyond facile framings of planned economies and the centralized state. Far from a "desert," the postsocialist terrain is rich with experiment, inspired by excavations of the past and enhanced by international and transversal connections in the present.[5]

With Midnight Notes, we see the horizon of commons/commoning as revolutionary possibility. While in our title we riff on Jodi Dean's *Communist Horizon*, we understand the horizon on different terms than Dean, who imagines it as a "dimension of experience" that we may "lose sight of" but "can never lose."[6] Our horizon is always in the making, standing at a remove from the centripetal certainty of the vanguard party's orientation. Commonist futurity begins from the priorities of immediate reproduction—life is not subordinated to a sacrificial politics which can only promise the good life as an idea, a longing, an outcome—the denunciation of *living* for

5. Srećko Horvat and Igor Štiks, eds., *Welcome to the Desert of Post-Socialism: Radical Politics After Yugoslavia* (London and New York: Verso, 2015); Iva Čukić and Jovana Timotijević, eds., *Spaces of Commoning: Urban Commons in the Ex-YU Region* (Belgrade: Ministry of Space/Institute for Urban Politics, 2020); Tomislav Tomašević, Vedran Horvat, Alma Midžić, Ivana Dragšić and Miodrag Dakić, *Commons in South East Europe: The Case of Croatia, Bosnia & Herzegovina and Macedonia* (Zagreb: Institute for Political Ecology, 2018); Vedrana Bibić, Andrea Milat, Srećko Horvat, and Igor Štiks, *The Balkan Forum: Situations, Struggles, Strategies* (Zagreb: Rosa Luxemburg Stiftung, 2014); Margit Mayer, Catharina Thörn, and Håkan Thörn, *Urban Uprisings: Challenging Neoliberal Urbanism in Europe* (London: Springer, 2016); Kerstin Jacobsson, ed., *Urban Grassroots Movements in Central and Eastern Europe* (Surrey: Ashgate, 2015).

6. Jodi Dean, *The Communist Horizon* (London and New York: Verso, 2012), 1.

life.[7] The commons is neither a retreat to the parochial or premodern, nor a mere opposition of the concrete and the abstract with the general and the particular. We start in the muck of our daily existence; the horizon emerges from our desire as we move through these conditions. Thinking with Félix Guattari and Gilles Deleuze, we can say that our horizon comes to view as a manifestation and enunciation of a collective desire.

From the concrete here and now, rooted in the practices of local institutions, "we walk" like the Zapatistas, "asking questions." As we near the horizon constituted by such desire, a new horizon appears. This book, then, is an artifact and tool of a conversation, as well as a collective enunciation of a commonist horizon. Weaving urban locations, activities, and positions with those whom we recognize and hold dear, it opens itself to a transversal becoming on different scales. Insofar as this book constitutes a collective enunciation of a commonist horizon, that horizon is complex and multivocal: always rooted in a locale, suggesting, in the place of a teleology, a set of practices and critiques that can be linked together through noncapitalist and anticapitalist commoning formations.

If commoning is emphatically not Communism (as any form of existing state socialism) its relationship with many historical and contemporary communisms is worth exploring. Peter Linebaugh writes:

> In the 1840s, then, 'communism' was the new name to express the revolutionary aspirations of proletarians. It pointed to the future. . . . [I]n contrast, the 'commons' belonged to the past, perhaps to the feudal era, when it was the last-ditch defense against extinction. Now in the twenty-first century the semantics of the two terms seem to be reversed, with communism belonging to the past of Stalinism, industrialization of agriculture, and militarism, while the commons belongs to an international debate about the planetary future of land, water, and subsistence for all. What is sorely needed in this debate so far is allegiance to the actual movement of the common people who have been enclosed and foreclosed but are beginning to disclose an alternative, open future.[8]

While provoking the question of a common "ism," this book's collective enunciation brings together a set of situated actor-thinkers to consider the

---

7. For a strong critique of the horizon as a modernist sacrificial teleology, see Massimiliano Tomba, *Marx's Temporalities* [*Historical Materialism* 44] (Leiden: Koninklijke Brill NV, 2013).

8. Peter Linebaugh, *Stop, Thief! The Commons, Enclosures, and Resistance* (Oakland: PM Press, 2014), 212.

commons as an idea, a practice, and strategy. Why then focus on capitalist *urbanization?* First, capital accumulation is closely tied to urbanization, to transformation of the built and natural environment in manners that are tied to tricks of finance and hasten the frequency of the crises we are experiencing. Second, more than half of the world's population lives in cities—we do too. As Linebaugh stresses, Marx and Engels focus on the political standpoint of landless urban commoners (proletarians), contributing to unfortunate distinctions, from today's lens, among the proletarian, lumpenproletarian, and peasantry.[9] Urban-rural migration brings the knowledges of people in the countryside to cities, while financial capital finds ways to accumulate (and defer crisis to the future) via the transformation of space, whether in land grabs in the countryside or "development" in the cities.

We consider urban commoning here because we begin our analysis with our own lives, in cities. But cities are not independent of the countryside. Rather, they are dependent in so many ways. Not only have urban labor struggles so often been supported by neighborhood and community organizations, but workers who produce the city range from those who provide food, to urban consumers, to those who mine the steel that girds the buildings.[10] "Unlike so many images of the worker as the champion of history, the commons blurs the boundary between production and social reproduction."[11] The urbanization of capital, so central to our moment, means that the capitalist class not only dominates the state but also the urban process itself, which affects rural regions too. In this context, the movements of the squares, right to the city movements, and urban uprisings can all be seen as struggles to appropriate urban space for common purposes.[12]

Other movements have taught us that the territory is a place of social reproduction of our communities and their resistances, insurrections, and insurgencies.[13] The commons can ask us, then, to consider our cities, neighborhoods, and districts as territory and ourselves as part of a social body

9. Linebaugh, *Stop, Thief!*, 212.

10. David Harvey, *Rebel Cities: From the Right to the City to the Urban Revolution* (London and New York: Verso, 2019), 132–133.

11. Harvey, *Rebel Cities*, 132–133.

12. Harvey, *Rebel Cities*, 132–133.

13. Raúl Zibechi, *Territories in Resistance: A Cartography of Latin American Social Movements* (Oakland: AK Press, 2012), 68–69; Massimiliano Tomba, *Insurgent Universality: An Alternative Legacy of Modernity* (New York: Oxford University Press, 2019), 212.

sustained by and sustaining this territory. But while territories may be conceived as commons, many commons are not (yet) territories. Commoning on a smaller scale, whether by teaching and learning skills and practices together, taking care of our collective, by tending to a community garden, or by caring for a shared project, is a starting point, even if we wish to expand to territories, solidarity economies, or confederations. "Commons" to us means commoning. Beyond a resource and its defense is also a social relation.

The Chapters, or *en avant pour le dérive!*

Emerging from a process initiated by the Naujininkai Commons Collective at Luna6 in Vilnius, this book carries the transversal connections shaped across multi-scale, multimodal movements and everyday formations.[14] The present volume is composed of five interventions by movement thinkers who were invited to take part in this project because they are already working together with the editors across multiple fields and actions. While this volume is restricted and enabled by the material conditions of the written page, we invite you to take a less determined journey through these urban landscapes of commons and their other(s) as a *dérive*. Moving through stylistic shifts and different positions, perhaps you will find some common ground and a commonist horizon.

Our dialogical process stretches to authors in capital cities of two other former state socialist republics: Budapest, Hungary and Belgrade, Serbia. From there we go to London, England and then, to a translocally constituted collective writing from New York City in *Lenapehoking*. Collectively, authors take up the lived experience of building what might be called "urban commons," offering insights on the conceptual and political potentials and limitations of this terminology and associated practices.

We begin with Ana Vilenica's **Who Has "The Right to Common"? Decolonizing Commoning in East Europe**. Writing from Serbia, Vilenica challenges the dominance of Western epistemologies to address how the neocolonial discourse of transition from state socialism to neoliberalism conveniently erased vital leftist histories of commoning/commons in former

---

14. You can find these discussions, readings, district dinners, and talks here: http://luna6.lt/naujininkai-commons/discussions.

socialist East Europe. Vilenica argues that the category of "social property" and the "self-managed" housing experiments in socialist Yugoslavia should be seen as commons, even if they are imperfect and contradictory forms. She goes on to identify how the neocolonial transition discourse erases these empowering legacies while enforcing divisive racialized attitudes in today's housing movement that have resulted in the failure to grasp critical opportunities for commoning. In Chapter 2, Anthony Iles' **From the Neoliberal City to Disaster Capitalism, from Commons to "Unenclosure"** explores the changing relation between urban development and the cultural field, bringing us along in a search for agency in the suffocating climate of contemporary London. Setting this relation within the history of "new enclosures" and the emergence of a commons discourse in the British New Left, Iles addresses how practices of so-called commoning have been used as "dressing" for real estate developers. Analyzing the critical shortcomings of these popular commoning formations, he makes an appeal for the commons as an antagonistic practice of *unenclosure*. The contribution includes a glossary of concepts on commons, which points to core concepts circulating throughout the book. In Chapter 3, **A Movement to Transform Everything: Knowledge Production Towards Solidarity Economy in Hungary**, Mary N. Taylor engages Zsuzsanna Pósfai (cofounder, Periféria Center) and Ágnes Gagyi (cofounder, Solidarity Economy Center) in a conversation on the processes of knowledge production and the political and economic conditions that led to their work developing cooperative rental housing in Budapest's postsocialist and financialized housing landscape. In Chapter 4, **Reclaiming Care in the Urban Commons**, the CareNotes Collective—writing from New York City—meditates on urban commons as transversally constituted processes of care work and social reproduction. Taking care as a central practice of building, the urban commons is seen as a process of overcoming the territorialized and alienated care relations in public and private and community health/care, made particularly urgent during the COVID-19 pandemic. Returning to where we started, in Vilnius, Naujininkai Commons (NC) closes the book with Chapter 5, **Capital's Social Fix: Divestment and Agency in the Post-Socialist Regenerate City**. Tracing the emergence of everyday agential formations in late-Soviet and post-Soviet Lithuania, NC analyzes the changing composition between semi-autonomous commoning practices, the state, and real estate developers. Seeing how commoning practices have been subsumed into real estate development strategies, they consider how threshold commoning and public-common partnerships (PCPs) can be used in strategic ways to constitute autonomous common infrastructures in their neighborhood, city, and region.

Chapter 1

WHO HAS "THE RIGHT TO COMMON"? DECOLONIZING COMMONING IN EAST EUROPE

Ana Vilenica

During the meeting of a European network of housing activists a few years ago, an activist from Serbia presented a contemporary urban initiative as "the first organization ever in the history of Serbia to prevent eviction." My attempt to argue otherwise brought an unexpectedly aggressive reaction from this person. At first this made me think about how little we know about our own history. On further thought, their sincere conviction made me wonder about whose struggles count as anti-eviction struggles in Serbia. Housing movements in Serbia are not new, as some activists have tried to present at public events and international activist meetings that I have attended over the years. There is a long tradition of commoning vacant land for housing and anti-eviction struggles, but they have been invisibilized because they don't belong to the Western European canon of struggles.

While the history of commoning and anti-eviction struggles in Serbia is yet to be written, research by Zlata Vuksanović-Macura and Vladimir Macura shows struggles for the right to housing in Serbia go back to the end of World War I. In 1918, squatter settlements emerged as a new phenomenon in Belgrade. When the City of Belgrade threatened to demolish the biggest squatters' settlement, known as "Jatagan-mala," residents fought fiercely against the eviction and for the monetary compensation they believed they had a right to upon being evicted.[1] Systematic disregard of these histories, and others that have followed in contemporary Serbia, point to the neocolonial "Western activist outlook" imposed by middle-class civil society organizations during the transition to capitalism and alleged "democratization" in Eastern Europe after the Yugoslav socialist experiment ended.

As with anti-eviction struggles, mainstream discussions on commons in both East and West Europe assume that emancipatory ideas of commons and commoning come from the West. However, socialist experiments in Eastern Europe have left us with a significantly different tradition and understanding these differences will enrich our knowledge on commons. Housing construction and its status as societal property in the Yugoslav system of self-management, along with its pitfalls and the commoning that addressed its gaps, offer important lessons for scaling up commons. Contemporary housing commoning in Serbia has unfolded against the background of an antisocialist housing transition and the individualization of responsibility for one's home, feeding unjust policies that contribute to increased housing repatriarchalization, racialization, precarity, and homelessness. Processes of commoning have been influenced by the market and the state, as well as by mobilizing the logics of activists and affected people on the ground.

Due to the historical revisionism aimed at creating anticommunist sentiment, commoning in Eastern Europe has to deal not only with inserting itself into Westernized narratives about commons but also with anticollectivist sentiments on the ground. Ideas of commons and commoning have also been subject to a certain idealization, romanticization, and uncritical representation in the writing about housing movements in Serbia. This can be understood as emerging from our attempt to include East European struggles into a Western canon of knowledge production on commons and commoning, while at the same time trying to overcome the general atmosphere of distrust towards collective projects imposed by neocolonial "transitional" narratives. To fully understand how commoning unfolds here, it is necessary to look at its paradoxes and contradictions.

---

1. Jatagan-mala is also known as "Jatagan Mala" and "Jatagan mahala." These all refer to the same former informal settlement in Belgrade inhabited by urban poor residents, including many Romani people. When the construction of a new highway through Belgrade began in the 1960s, the population of Jatagan-mala was displaced and the neighborhood was demolished.

In this chapter, I show how postwar commons-making and common-ing in East Europe has been disregarded, while stressing that commoning here requires a more nuanced analysis. Understanding postwar histories of commoning and commons asks for a complex decolonial approach that would include these questions: how do we simultaneously address the legacies of East Europe's colonial past and the fact that East Europe has been colonized within the capitalist modern world system? How do we reckon with the limited nature of self-managed societal housing and the simultaneous existence of informal housing solutions in Yugoslavia? How do we build a left decolonial approach from the East when the right loudly articulates an anticolonial position? How do we move away from "saving the poor" approaches and toward learning lessons from alternative practices of the struggle for homes. What remains clear is that ignoring the complex (post) Yugoslav housing histories, the classed, racialized, and gendered contradictions of activists, and the informal networks of commoning in illegalized spaces will only result in missed opportunities to inscribe counter-histories, based in experience, into the insurgent path towards another future.

The Case for a Yugoslav "Housing Commons"

From a conversation with an architect to activist scholar conferences on commoning to our everyday activist work, I have witnessed with anger, over and over again, how the region's transition to capitalism operates. In particular, how it requires the negation of our histories. In March 2019, at a seminar with Stavros Stavrides in Belgrade entitled "Rethinking Housing as Urban Commons," a well-known professor discussed the intersection of (Western) commons theory with movements that are pursuing visions of the "just city" in postsocialist Belgrade. At the end of the round of presentations, I asked her if ideas and practices of socially owned and to some extent self-managed housing in Yugoslavia, even with all of its pitfalls, could be seen as a commons or commoning. She was categorical that it was far from commoning yet acknowledged there are conceptual overlaps that were attractive even to Henri Lefebvre, who spoke about Yugoslavia's particular place in "urban revolution" in a lecture when visiting Yugoslavia. In her opinion, while the housing that came under the category of societal property was attractive as a concept, its real world application took a different shape. To complement her standpoint, another activist-researcher confirmed that what happened in the Yugoslav period was definitely not commoning; not simply because self-management failed in so many respects but because housing practices were very idealistic. As an example of commoning, he introduced the tradition maintained by people who had moved to the cities from rural parts of the country of grilling peppers for winter on the balconies of their socialist tower blocks. In his opinion, the urban population should have seen this practice as commoning, while in fact they saw it as something that doesn't belong to the city. While urban-rural hierarchies are not to be neglected, this simplified scenario fails to take the socialist experiment seriously.

How do we explain Yugoslav housing commoning to a person unconsciously (self-) colonized by Western narratives about East Europe, whose process of learning has been blocked by a very rigid black-and-white and often simplified picture of the past? Let's start from a few facts. Yugoslav socialist self-management was born after the break with Stalin in the *Informbiro* period beginning in mid-1948. The subsequent necessity to overcome isolation from both the East and West, in many respects, contributed to the invention of the historically new form of "societal property" [*društvena svojina*].[2] Although many have underlined how self-management was introduced from the top down, it is important to keep in mind that the state was understood as a transitional form meant to serve as guarantor of the socialist character of reforms until dissolving into the communes; that is, into associations of direct producers. The housing system in Yugoslavia was flexible, allowing many forms, scales, and modalities of practices. It constantly evolved due to continuing reforms over time, further complicating our research and understanding of this system.[3] Housing was decommodified in Yugoslavia in 1945, forbidding anyone to own more than one residence. Housing surplus was nationalized in 1958, and in 1968, all land became socially owned.

Due to the dire state of the housing stock after World War II, Yugoslav society mobilized its own human resources through worker and youth brigades. Voluntary labor actions of workers and youth were organized on

---

2. We use societal property here to translate *društvena svojina*. This "third" property form in socialist Yugoslavia was neither "public" (i.e., "social") nor "private," but socially owned and managed. We use societal instead of social to distinguish it from "social property," which elsewhere means "public property," especially when referring to "social housing."

3. Jelica Jovanović, "Materializing the Self-Management: Tracking the Commons in Yugoslav Housing," in *Housing as Commons: Housing Alternatives as Response to the Current Urban Crisis*, ed. Stavros Stavrides and Penny Travlou, np (London: Bloomsbury, forthcoming).

local, republic, and federal levels by the Yugoslav Communist League to build public infrastructures in the form of roads, railways, buildings, and industrial infrastructure. Existing practices such as local brickyard production served as a bases for the new construction industry that in coming decades became a site of experimentation with modular prefabrication systems that were highly flexible, transformable, and transportable, alongside experiments with floor plans.[4] Some of these are still in use today. The focus of the hybrid housing economy was on the production and distribution of housing stock, the responsibility over which moved in time from the state and municipalities to socialist enterprises and worker's councils. Workers partly self-financed the socially owned housing stock with an obligatory contribution to the housing fund used to place workers in flats according to a ranking list. Until the end of Yugoslavia—at the beginning of the 1990s—less than one-fourth of housing across the entire country was socially owned. Ownership of individual housing had been tolerated throughout Yugoslavia's socialist period, and there was also a small percentage of social housing for very disadvantaged people.

Due to the chronic lack of housing, especially in urban centers, many took things into their own hands and constructed their own housing, mostly on agricultural land in the tolerated gray zone of housing provision on the outskirts of cities, aided by favorable loans from the state for construction materials. Traditional rural forms such as *moba* were invoked to rebuild and develop. Moba, rooted in customary law and considered to be a long-term collective loan, was used traditionally as a mobilization strategy of villagers in home construction. Until the 1980s, informal construction in Serbia accounted for one-third of all buildings.[5] This type of construction emerged in the gaps between what was systematically declared, institutionally established, and actually practiced.[6]

Informal construction became an alternative method of achieving the right to housing by means of self-organization.[7] This occurred with "silent"

---

4. Jovanović, "Materializing the Self-Management."

5. See Slavka Zeković, Ksenija Petovar, and Bin Md Saman Nor-Hisham, "The credibility of illegal and informal construction: Assessing legalization policies in Serbia," *Cities* 97 (2020): 1–12.

6. Zeković, Petovar, and Saman, "The credibility of illegal and informal construction."

7. Slavka Zeković, Tamara Maričić, and Marija Cvetinović, "Transformation of Housing Policy in a Post-Socialist City: The Example of Belgrade," in *Regulating the City: Contemporary Urban Housing*, ed. Julian Sidoli, Marvin Noah Frank Kiehl, and Michel Vols (The Hague: Eleven International Publishing, 2017), 41–64.

or temporary permission of formal institutions mostly in periurban areas, on public construction land, and in public areas. Some of the settlements in periurban areas later demanded infrastructure from the municipality, further adding to the interplay of tensions in the "revolutionary process." For example, between the mid-1970s and the mid-1980s, the Belgrade neighborhood of Kaludjerica organized to win bus service, running water pipes, primary schools, and a health center.[8]

Revolutionizing the structures of socioeconomic relations in the sphere of territorial development also included new models of organization—the territorial-political self-management of local communities.[9] Following Yugoslavia's communal system rooted in the people's committees of the antifascist national liberation struggle, the municipality (commune) was established as the basic sociopolitical community. In the beginning, this system was critical towards both bourgeois concepts of local self-management and anarcho-utopic conceptions of the commune. The functioning of new forms of economic (workers' councils) and territorial-political self-government implied wide democratic participation of citizens in the decision-making process. This was meant to suppress centralist and bureaucratic tendencies in the management of socioeconomic processes, and gradually overcome regional inequalities in economic development, as well as the opposition of villages and cities.[10] Urban self-management clearly never reached its ideal form in Yugoslavia, but it was partially realized at the micro level of local housing units and to a lesser extent at the level of urban and architectural planning.

Significant research has revealed pitfalls of the Yugoslav housing distribution system and its self-management, including manipulation of the ranking list to prioritize white collar workers and technocrats and the emergence of a new socialist upper-class with multiple homes.[11] Little has been written, however, about the racialized and gendered aspects of

---

8. Ana Džokić and Marc Neelan, "Walks on the Wild Side," in *Concurrent Urbanities: Designing Infrastructures of Inclusion*, ed. Miodrag Mitrašinovic (New York and Milton Park, Abingdon, Oxon: Routledge, 2016), 37–60.

9. Milan Rakita, *Prostorno-političke i memorijalne infrastrukture socijalističke Jugoslavije* (Belgrade: Rosa Luxemburg Stiftung Southeast Europe, 2020).

10. Rakita, *Prostorno-političke*, 24.

11. Rory Archer, "'Imaš kuću—vrati stan.' Housing inequalities, socialist morality and discontent in 1980s Yugoslavia," *Godišnjak za društvenu istoriju* [*Annual of Social History*] 20, no. 3 (2015): 119–139; Rory Archer, "The moral economy of home construction in late socialist Yugoslavia," *History and Anthropology* 29, no. 2 (2018): 141–162.

FIGURE 1.1. *Demolition of a house somewhere in Vojvodina [autonomous province comprising northern Serbia] with a bust of Tito in the stucco decoration on the last standing wall. Photo by Mihajlo Vujasin.*

housing dynamics in Yugoslavia. Urbanization and urban planning during the socialist experiment restructured social relations, especially traditional gender roles. Massive rural-urban migration made cities a strategic place of women's emancipation.[12] Patriarchal ideology cohabitated with the new ideology of equality within the household as well as in allegedly "gender-blind" urban development and planning. The double burden faced by women was addressed by the socialization of the means of social reproduction such as childcare, elder care, and cooking, but was limited to employed urban women only. The socialization of the work to support these networks and their reproduction was borne by women of different generations, often preventing them from migrating to cities. The shortage of apartments contributed to increased cohabitation of extended families. In this sense, for many women, housing was, unintendedly, a direct obstacle to emancipation.

In the region, Yugoslavia was considered to have one of the most progressive policies towards the Roma population.[13] Unlike other socialist countries in Eastern Europe, the Yugoslav government never attempted a collective resettlement of Roma. However, principles of equality in housing improved the lives of only a very small proportion of Roma people. While sedentarization was enforced by the requirement of a fixed place of residence, the societal housing option distributed by self-managed enterprises was affected by Roma underrepresentation in the formal employment that was the path to this form of housing provision.[14] Furthermore, those Roma practicing more traditional values found the layout of the socialist apartment objectionable to their way of life. All this led to a preference among Roma for self-building.

12. Ana Pajvancic-Cizelj and Marina Hjuson, "Urbanization and Urban Planning at the European Semi-Periphery: Unintended Gender Consequences," *Sociologija*, no. 1 (2018): 279.

13. Alma Huselj, *Lost in Transition: The Legacies of Yugoslav Policies on Serbian Roma's Housing Insecurities* (Undergraduate Senior Thesis, Princeton University, 2019), 3.

14. Huselj, *Lost in Transition*, 15.

While the segregation of Roma in *"mahalas"*[15] was a pattern that emerged before socialist Yugoslavia, similar housing conditions continued to exist in Yugoslav times. Despite a focus on education and occupational competence, the issue of housing in Roma settlements was completely neglected, only to be raised in the 1980s as a problem of illegality.[16] Due to the decentralized nature of governance, the Yugoslav housing system has experienced great variation throughout the country. In all regions, there were many who fell through the cracks between socialist policy and the informal solutions that functioned to buffer its systemic incapacity to deal with the ongoing housing crisis.[17]

There is no doubt that historic socialist Yugoslav housing solutions, formal and informal, offer important lessons for commoning. Tracing this history in Yugoslavia is a work of unveiling complex interactions among Yugoslav workers, the governance of a state meant to die out, and "socialist" and market forces, as they took shape in the experiments of self-management and social housing in tension with micro-commoning and self-help that emerged through informal solutions. Contradictions emerging in the process of Yugoslav housing solutions indisputably bear important lessons about potentialities and pitfalls of scaling up housing commons. Among these lessons are those pertaining to the invisibilized issues of gender and race.

---

15. The concept of *"Tsigane ma'la/mahala"* or *"Roma mahala"* is used in this article to denote informalized, legalized, and improvised living infrastructures inhabited mostly by diverse groups such as Roma(ni), Egyptians, Gypsy, Ashkali, and other urban-poor dwellers. These formations are racialized and either located at the outskirts of cities and villages or in the secluded areas within the city core. The material conditions of living in mahala are usually scarcity and precarity. Although they live under the constant threat of eviction and/or racialized violence, the inhabitants of mahalas have managed to survive on scanty resources and improvised infrastructure for centuries. In fact, the term *mahala* or "mahalle" originates from the Arabic word for "settlement" or "quarters" and it has been introduced into the Balkan settings with the arrival of the Ottomans in the 15th century. Today, its meaning is derogatory as it approximates the terms "ghetto" or "slum" and almost invariably refers to Roma mahalas. See Ana Vilenica and Ivana Pražić, "Why All of 'Us' Are Challenged to Struggle against 'Whiteness,'" *Berliner Gazette*, December 13, 2021, https://blogs.mediapart.fr/berliner-gazette/blog/131221/black-box-east-why-all-us-are-challenged-struggle-against-whiteness.

16. Zlata Vuksanović-Macura, "Spatial Segregation of Roma Settlements within Serbian Cities. Examples from Belgrade, Novi Sad, and Kruševac," in *Spatial Conflicts and Divisions in Post-socialist Cities*, ed. Valentin Mihaylov (New York: Springer, 2020), 213.

17. Huselj, *Lost in Transition*, 20.

Dispossession of the Yugoslav Commons

As I write, mass protests are taking place all around Serbia against the new law on expropriation of land proposed in the National Assembly to aid the multinational British-Australian corporation Rio Tinto in setting up a new lithium mine in Western Serbia. The corporation intends to buy the homes and land of twenty-two villages near the city of Loznica. People in Serbia are aware of what a disaster this corporation has been for the environment and people all around the world—from the extreme pollution of water in Madagascar and Papua New Guinea to the destruction of Aboriginal caves in Australia. Many peasants in the region have agreed to sell their fertile ancestral land and their homes. The price was good, but it is hard to buy something as good with that money. Others are staying put, firmly stating that Rio Tinto can have their land only over their dead bodies. Despite their resistance, the area looks devastated. Houses that have been sold stand empty behind red-and-white ribbon. Many are without roofs, mostly because former inhabitants were able to take everything they wanted, including construction material, from the houses.

In Serbia, foreign investment is promoted as a development strategy. It is supposedly a solution to all our problems, despite numbers that clearly point to the fact that investors are here only to take. Rio Tinto has been the last straw. I recently watched a video report produced by an ultra-nationalist independent online media outlet, in which the male voice floating over images of devastated houses sharply criticizes "the new colonizers" who will "make Serbs into slaves," "just like in the Third World countries." To describe this land and housing grab, he states: "They are making a state within state . . . a little Kosovo in Serbia." Initially I was struck by surprise, but quickly remembered there is nothing new about this narrative. Although this right-wing anticolonial discourse speaks to real inequalities in the global distribution of economic and political power, it does so by reproducing nationalistic Serbian "internal" imperialism against Albanians, Muslims, and Roma, as well as people from other geographies who are perceived as outsiders.

Many Marxists who understood primitive accumulation as a one-time historical event, by the 1990s had come to realize primitive accumulation is a process that is integral to capitalism at all times. In the 1990s, the entirety of East Europe—including ex-Yugoslavia—became the class-divided, racialized, and ghettoized site of "transitional enclosure" of land, housing, technologies, ideas, and lives. Economic crises, paired with nationalistic tensions and interventions by the "international community" (UN, EU, NATO, etc.), led to the tragic outcomes of wars lasting nearly a decade (1991–2001).

In the domain of housing, the process of dispossession started with ethnic cleansing across the borders of the ex-Yugoslav republics. Serbia still refuses to admit its official role in the imperialist wars on the territories of other Yugoslav republics, not to mention, the systematic denial of the genocide of the Muslim population in Bosnia and Herzegovina and the mass graves of Albanians discovered in Serbia in recent years. In 1996, Serbia registered 537,937 refugees, mostly from Bosnia and Herzegovina and Croatia, and 200,000 internally displaced persons from the war in Kosovo.[18] This mass exchange of populations across the borders of ex-Yugoslav republics was coeval with massive privatization of the societal housing stock. It was transferred to the state and made state property to allow for privatization. During this process, beginning in 1992, inhabitants were encouraged to purchase their homes, once socially owned property, from the state at subsidized prices—thus providing the state with funds to finance the wars. For many, ownership of the space one lived in was soon to become a kind of "asset-based welfare," a last resource for survival after war, cycles of inflation, bank-led pyramid scheme frauds, unemployment, and poverty. State-owned housing stock, once societal property, was diminished to less than 1 percent.

Privatization and restitution were represented in mainstream narratives as the "path to democracy" and "property freedom" after a supposedly messy period of property as "everyone's and no one's." In the coming years, multiple housing crises emerged from these changes and the commodification and financialization of housing, leaving many in precarity. A large number of young people, including myself, were forced to live with extended family or rent in the overpriced "gray" rental housing market. The urban poor were forced to squat land and abandoned housing for survival. At the same time, the implementation of restitution was set as a condition for Serbia's (not yet successful) accession to the European Union. Most homes eligible for restitution came with sitting tenants whose rights have been gradually diminished. While the Yugoslav working class moved into apartments as

---

18. See Commissariat for Refugees and Migration Republic of Serbia, https://kirs.gov.rs/eng.

a political and collective subject of a society that at least nominally had radical equality—you could even say commoning—as its vision, this same subject has been forced to move out of them, humiliated and delegitimized as individualized "welfare cases."[19]

Both privatization of housing and restitution are violent processes of replacement of socialist housing infrastructure with new/old ownership regimes that have made segments of the working class into "losers." Among the losers were those who had been using housing that couldn't be privatized, including temporary worker's accommodations and property nationalized in the 1950s, and those with insufficient funds to purchase the premises they were living in. The criminal privatization of socialist enterprises, first bankrupted and then sold to tycoons under burgeoning prices, often included worker's barracks. Ex-workers, sold together with their companies, have since been evicted or live under threat of eviction.

Neoliberal urban development has reproduced old inequalities and created new ones, among them the loss of the previously acquired social position of women.[20] Contemporary Serbian urbanism, in its "gender-blind phase," reproduces gender inequalities in the home-ownership rate as well as failing to give women who are victims of domestic violence access to social housing services. In Serbia, women own only 13.95 percent of real estate, and only 14.65 percent own their own homes in a country with a more than 87 percent ownership rate.[21] The fact that many women are forced to stay at home in violent relationships and risk their lives only recently came into the focus of public policy through projects such as the European Union Support to Social Housing and Active Inclusion Programme (EU SHAI).

Additionally, the dissolution of Yugoslavia and the new "ethnification of politics"[22] has meant increased precarity for a large number of Roma people. Most Roma people were unable to practice the "right to buy" or legalize property due to a combination of the failures of the Yugoslav system with new property regimes. Many informal Roma settlements have

19. See Mapping Against Restitutions, https://fundaction.eu/project/mapping-against-restitutions/.

20. Pajvančić-Cizelj and Blagojević, "Urbanization and Urban Planning at the European Semi-Periphery," 282.

21. Vedrana Lacmanović and Aleksandra Nestorov, *Politika socijalnog stanovanja: Mogućnosti i stvaranje prava za žene koje su preživele nasilje* (Belgrade: Autonomni ženski centar, 2021).

22. István Pogány, "Pariah Peoples: Roma and the Multiple Failures of Law in Central and Eastern Europe," *Social & Legal Studies* 21, no. 3 (2012): 384.

become illegal due to new property rights essential to capitalist urbanism. They are under constant threat of demolition and eviction due to the pursuit of profitable land by investors, in a situation in which discrimination is multilayered. Roma face municipal and court decisions that deprive them of their rights to housing support.[23] In the rare cases in which social housing has been granted to Roma families, it has not been an acceptable solution. After they were finally evicted from the contested territory of New Belgrade in 2012, displaced Romani people were moved to container settlements on the outskirts of the city in marshlands lacking basic infrastructure. Many have remained there until today, partly due to concessions made to middle-class residents who rebelled against accommodations for displaced Roma being built in their neighborhood. The "lucky" ones ended up in social housing—state-owned submarket rentals that are unaffordable to them—and now face eviction due to accumulated debt.[24]

In the last thirty years, investor-led urbanism has foregrounded the interests of investors over those of the public, and "splintered"[25] socialist planning into opportunities to accumulate capital. Extralegal construction characterized housing production in the 1990s, with 43 percent of housing said to be built without permission in 2017. In the second decade of the twenty-first century, negotiating the legal and extralegal became an important instrument of the state in bringing about megaprojects such as the Belgrade Waterfront—an elite district with housing prices unaffordable for the impoverished citizens of Serbia. Instead of enlarging the social housing sector, Serbia went for finance-led welfare, subsidizing bank loans for specific groups such as public sector workers and military personnel. The rest were left to solve their housing issues on the newly financialized housing market with often toxic financial assets. This has led to an unprecedented debt crisis for those that took out such predatory housing loans.[26]

Serbia has become a regional center of money laundering through the housing market: less than 20 percent was bought through bank loans, while more than 80 percent of housing was purchased with cash. Keeping in

---

23. Macura, "Spatial Segregation of Roma Settlements within Serbia," 221.

24. Ana Vilenica, "Contradictions and Antagonisms in (Anti-) Social(ist) Housing in Serbia," *ACME: An International Journal for Critical Geographies* 18, no. 6 (December 2019): 1261–1282.

25. Simon Marvin and Steve Graham, *Splintering Urbanism: Networked Infrastructures, Technological Mobilities and the Urban Condition* (Oxford: Routledge, 2001).

26. For instance, more than 20,000 people took a housing loan indexed in CHF and became victims of predatory foreign bank lending practices at the (semi)periphery of Europe.

FIGURE 1.2. *Distant view of the Belgrade Waterfront project from Kalemegdan Fortress, and the newly built waterfront tower across the river, as seen from the former Belgrade fairground site—where the Sajmište concentration camp was located during WWII. Photo by Ana Vilenica.*

mind the average salary in Serbia doesn't exceed 500 euros per month, the origins of the money invested in housing rings an alarm.

Such criminal structures in Serbia provide themselves with the support of global capital through foreign investments from old and new centers of economic and political power that have, in parallel, shaped new regimes of housing. The intensification of housing precarity is connected to megaprojects such as the Belgrade Waterfront, a public-private partnership (PPP) involving a company from the United Arab Emirates. This project has displaced more than 200 families, offering only temporary housing solutions to some. All this is happening as Serbia continues to export a cheap labor force to Western Europe, while at home, an even cheaper migrant labor force—mostly from Asia—is brutally exploited. An example is the Ling Long Company rubber factory, relocated to the city of Zrenjanin in 2018 from the People's Republic of China because of the pollution. It was recently exposed that workers from Vietnam employed by Ling Long in Zrenjanin live in slave-like conditions. Their passports are taken from them, and their movement is restricted to the company's construction site, where they "live" in dire hygienic conditions without electricity or sufficient food.

In the name of making the court system "efficient," as a condition for accession in the EU, the state recently privatized the work of bailiffs as a solution for the enforcement of court verdicts. This reform gave bailiffs public authority but requires them to finance themselves through "service" fees. The state introduced bailiffs as a promise of justice to those who lost jobs in the "transition" when companies were bankrupted and to whom new owners still owe back pay. However, the high costs of bailiff services made them unaffordable to the majority of impoverished people in Serbia, bringing benefits only to the middle class and those who profit from this system: sales agents, auction hosts, moving companies, locksmiths, and private security firms. Bailiffs have the power to decide how debt will be repaid. As a practice, they have been selling people's homes to make them pay off debts of a few thousand euros. Bailiffs are responsible for estimating the price of homes sold at auctions, where they sell at prices much lower than market value to people close to them. People are evicted today for many different reasons—including restitution, privatization of worker's accommodations, debt due to banks and loan sharks, overdue micro-loan payments and utility bills, frauds including investors selling the same flat to different people two or more times, as well as appropriation of land and "empty" premises used for housing purposes, mostly by Roma.

The imposition of "transition" to East European countries in the name of EU enlargement has long been identified as a neocolonial process.[27] In this process Eastern Europe became the other to be modernized by the West via neoliberal shock therapy that played out through the privatization and financialization of land and housing. This has led to further social inequalities and repatriarchalization and racialization of the newly established countries that emerged after the disintegration of Yugoslavia. New global dynamics of labor markets and resource exploitation, including migration and the production of borders, enacted by old and new global actors, additionally complicate contemporary housing regimes. Yet internal forms of domination in Serbia that combine with Western European neocolonialism are also important to address. Without a perspective on Roma, Albanians, Muslims, and the new global migrant labor force the image of contemporary dispossession in Serbia will not be complete.[28] The reactionary answer from right-wing critics of Europe's neocolonialism has yet to be met with a complex answer from the left. This answer needs to be, as Eszter Kováts formulates so well, "less tabooizing (in form of accusations similar to arguments of the Right) and more critical engagement with the inequalities that underpin the societal demands skillfully fuelled by the Right." Politically, she continues, "we need, instead of 'resistance' to their polarizing and stigmatizing discourse, effective organizing that addresses the root causes, the real economic and symbolic inequalities."[29]

Defining the Commons after Yugoslavia

A few months ago, I was struck—but not surprised—by a discussion on social media after the Roma theorist of racism, Jelena Savić, directed a critique at the campaign of a prominent Serbian feminist organization. In her

---

27. József Böröcz and Melinda Kovács, *Empire's New Clothes: Unveiling EU Enlargement* (Central Europe Review e-books, 2001), http://aei.pitt.edu/144/.

28. "Digital Lecture with Dr. Piro Rexhepi on European B/orders along the Balkan Refugee Route," moderated by Melina Borčak, March 25, 2021, https://www.youtube.com/watch?v=QyYQkx5uogg.

29. Eszter Kováts, "Black Block East: Right-Wing Anti-Colonialism and Universalising Postcolonialism," *Berliner Gazette*, December 12, 2021, https://blogs.mediapart.fr/berliner-gazette/blog/221221/black-box-east-right-wing-anti-colonialism-and-universalising-postcolonialism.

blog post "Anti-mahala feminism?" Savić notes how Roma mahalas always appear as spaces of shame from which Roma women need to be saved, and how there are "always 'color-blind' saviors" in this game. This criticism has been repeatedly dismissed along the usual "white feminism" lines of argumentation that promote European white supremacy through gender equality efforts. I have been thinking about how genealogies of informality and illegality are never discussed in these color-blind activist spaces, and about the contemporary East European "racial exceptionalism" that has emerged from recognizing that East Europeans are never quite allowed the status of "full whiteness."[30] I am also thinking about how commoning in mahalas remains a collection of stubborn forms, places, and practices of endurance and survival that buffer against racialized violence and constant threat of eviction as well as colonization by various kinds of "saintly activists," ranging from humanitarian to feminist. I co-wrote, with Ivana Pražić, two articles about alleged solidarity with Roma and its performativity. While the one in English was published, the one in Serbian never saw the light of day.[31] It was rejected by a leftist media outlet with a short comment: "it is not constructive enough."

Various contemporary movement formations draw from the history of the Yugoslav experiment, responding to its neoliberal aftermaths in the present. Movement scholars and scholar activists coming from the ex-Yugoslav region have made sporadic interventions in the Western canon of commons thinking by looking at self-management and societal property as commoning grounds. In 2013, at a time when "transition fatigue" began to fade, opening space for new progressive movements in East Europe, Danijela Dolenc and Mislav Žitko performed an exercise to strengthen commons theory and social struggles alike, summoning Elinor Ostrom's advocacy for commons governance principles as complementary to the state and market, and by drawing on Branko Horvat's theory of self-management to argue against both capitalism and statism.[32]

30. See József Böröcz, "'Eurowhite' Conceit, 'Dirty White' Resentment: 'Race' in Europe," *Sociological Forum* 36, no. 4 (December 2021): 1116–1134; Oleana Lyubchenko, "On the Frontier of Whiteness? Expropriation, War, and Social Reproduction in Ukraine," *LeftEast* (April 30, 2022), https://lefteast.org/frontiers-of-whiteness-expropriation-war-social-reproduction-in-ukraine/.
31. Vilenica and Pražić, "Why All of 'Us' are Challenged to Struggle against 'Whiteness.'"
32. Daniela Dolenec and Mislav Žitko, "Ostrom and Horvat: Identifying Principles of a Socialist Governmentality," *Grupa 22 Working Paper Series* (2013), www.grupa22.hr.

FIGURE 1.3. *A painting with a scene from the antifascist struggle during WWII leans against the outside wall of the house after its occupants are evicted. Photo by Ana Vilenica.*

For Horvat, self-managed socialist enterprise in Yugoslavia was meant to operate as a federation of self-governing communes—the same idea that Marx developed based on the history of the Paris Commune. Drawing on valuable local heritage, Dolenc and Žitko aimed to make space for the contemporary left to claim a new political posture toward socialism as an alternative to the prevalent liberal governmentality. Following this stream of thought, in 2016 Gal Kirn wrote an article entitled "Forgotten History of the Commons in Socialist Yugoslavia," where he emphasized societal ownership as a historical example largely ignored by the literature on the commons.[33] He criticizes well-established authors such as Hardt and Negri for dismissing socialism(s) in East Europe as a historical failure, a totalitarian deadlock, and a false alternative. Showing similarities with ways commons are described, Kirn discusses the paradox of Yugoslav self-management by examining the infrastructure of independent filmmaking in the space between amateur film clubs and large Yugoslav's film studios. In an inconclusive conclusion, he shows how building autonomy and self-organizing cultural production in Yugoslavia actually meant introducing more market-based and more capitalist forms of self-financing.

Despite these earlier interventions, recognition of our local history when thinking about commons and commoning generally remains limited, even while there have been some cases of a perhaps overenthusiastic application of commons language. In 2018, a group of researchers affiliated with Serbia's Institute for Political Ecology published *Commons in South East Europe* with the hope that the commons could become a political paradigm uniting progressive social movements in the region. The authors look at contemporary movements in Croatia, Bosnia and Herzegovina, and Macedonia dedicated to resisting privatization of natural resources and public services from the perspective of the commons. They approach commoning as a practice of governance consisting of resources, community, and institutions in a mutual relationship. Although the shared Yugoslav history of these countries is an explicit choice, there is no mention of commons and commoning in Yugoslavia in the volume's short history of commons from classical antiquity to modern times. The authors do, however, acknowledge how practices of collective management have been poorly researched in

---

33. Gal Kirn, "Forgotten History of the Commons in Socialist Yugoslavia: A Case of Self-Managed Cultural Infrastructure in the Period of 1960s and 1970s," *TkH Journal for Performing Art Theory* 23 (April 2016): 62–70.

the region due to nationalist forces which declared them a part of so-called Yugoslav totalitarianism. This legacy is presented as a major obstacle to any form of collective governance because it prompts negative public perceptions of forms—such as the cooperative—as connected with socialist totalitarianism. Continuing this work, the Ministry of Space collective published *Spaces of Commoning: Urban Commons in the Ex-YU Region* (2020). The case studies focus on former Yugoslav countries that were not covered in the 2018 volume: Serbia, Kosovo, and Montenegro. The authors position themselves within the critical theory of the commons and in relation to Ostrom's work on socialist governmentality, while also focusing on struggles and practices of commoning. In contrast to the 2018 publication, these authors acknowledge the proximity of Yugoslav self-management and the conceptual framework of commons.

A conversation about commons and commoning in housing in Serbia has been underway for some time in green social democratic circles, financed mostly by political foundations with a green agenda such as Germany's Heinrich Böll Foundation. These actors have been interested in housing as a potential material common good that is neither privately nor publicly owned as well as in issues of access and management in the midst of specific postsocialist housing crises, with a special focus on housing cooperatives.[34] This interest in commoning has recently entered spaces focused on anti-eviction, especially what is probably the most prominent activist organization: Joint Action "Roof Over Head" [*Združena akcija "Krov nad glavom"*] also known as "the Roof," founded in 2017 as a coalition of left-leaning organizations and a political party, the Social Democratic Union (SDU).[35]

In an article about the Roof, Jovana Timotijević from the Ministry of Space writes that although the concept of commons was never part of the Roof's discourse, it has certainly been an ideological framework of its advocacy practices.[36] The Roof has advocated for the de-privatization and de-commodification of housing, as well as the promotion of housing

---

34. See Iva Čukić, ed., *Kako zajednički do krova nad glavom: prilog kreiranju stambenih politika u Srbiji* (Belgrade: Mikro Art, 2018); Pametnija Zgrada [Smarter Building], https://www.pametnijazgrada.rs.

35. In 2020, the SDU merged into the Party of the Radical Left.

36. Jovana Timotijević, "Joint Action Roof Over Head," in *Spaces of Commoning: Urban Commons in the Ex-YU Region*, ed. Iva Čukić and Jovana Timotijević (Ministry of Space/Institute for Urban Politics, 2020), 96–107.

as a public infrastructure and right in pursuit of the common interest. Timotijević also argues that the organization functions as a commons through its implementation of radical democracy in decision-making processes, "through treating all of its resources as commons, including the knowledge that is produced throughout the process; and finally, through being radically open as a community itself, pushing for solidarity as its core principle and asset."[37]

In 2021, I—together with Vladimir Mentus and Irena Ristić (all of us members of the Roof at the time)—interpreted the work of the anti-eviction movement under COVID-19 pandemic conditions as commoning.[38] We described practices occurring during this period as temporary infra-commoning, connecting knowledge production, affect, care, food distribution, and housing in a politicized infrastructure, beyond merely filling in the gaps of the nonfunctional system.[39] It could be said that what we wrote about housing commons and commoning in both of these articles was subject to a certain idealization, romanticization, and uncritical representation as we attempted to simultaneously include East Europe's struggles into a Western canon of knowledge production on commons and commoning, and to overcome the general atmosphere of distrust towards collective projects due to dominant "transition" narratives on the ground. To fully understand how commoning unfolds, as well as the way we think about it, we must insist on looking at blind spots, paradoxes, and contradictions. Commoning is an imperfect process that is full of potential mistakes and often risks falling into exclusionary or hierarchical traps.

Housing Commons: Contradictions Towards Futures

I joined the emerging anti-eviction movement in 2009 as a member of Belgrade's cultural scene attempting to become allies of Romani people struggling against eviction in New Belgrade's Bellville settlement. Several cultural, student, and political organizations formed the "Anti-Wire" initiative—referring to how, during the 2009 Summer Universiade (World

---

37. Timotijević, "Joint Action Roof Over Head," 106.

38. Ana Vilenica, Vladimir Mentus, and Irena Ristić, "Struggles for Care Infrastructures in Serbia: The Pandemic, Dispossessed Care, and Housing," *Historical Social Research* 46, no. 4 (December 2021): 189–208.

39. Kelly Dombroski, Gradon Diprose, and Irene Boles, "Can the Commons be Temporary? The Role of Transitional Commoning in Post-Quake Christchurch," *Local Environment* 24, no. 4 (January 2019): 313–328.

University Summer Games), hosted by the city of Belgrade near Bellville, the settlement was fenced in with wire and hidden behind banners. Anti-Wire's purpose was to fight against racism directed at Romani people and the eviction of people in this settlement that was, at the time, sitting in the path of an infrastructural project of European importance, funded by the European Union and the profitable development of New Belgrade, led by local tycoons and foreign banks.

During the Summer Universiade, journalists and athletes were told that what was beyond the wire fence was the set for a new movie by famous director (of films often featuring Roma) Emir Kusturica. During this time, I was welcomed into the homes of people in the settlement, who told me stories about how families have been living there for many decades. They shared with me how the settlement had grown during the wars in the 1990s, and especially during the war in Kosovo when many people had to flee because they were neither Serbs nor Albanians. Some didn't speak Serbian because they had grown up in Germany only to be deported by force under the readmission agreement Serbia signed with the EU in order to qualify for membership. Many residents of Bellville had no documents or were unable to ask for benefits because they have been denied the status extended to other victims of the wars.

Housing dispossession produces violence and suffering, but it can also become grounds for material and immaterial "contentious practices" crucial for maintaining life in struggle.[40] Though the term is not strongly embedded in the vocabulary of movements, there have been attempts to describe housing struggles and their outcomes in Serbia as "commoning."[41] Housing

---

40. Civic engagement in Serbia has been looked at from the perspective of democratization theory, "as a source of social capital, political habits, and civic skills that are necessarily prerequisite for a stable democracy, and active grassroots organizing as a way of directly influencing the political process." Consequently, anti-authoritarian "colored revolutions" and liberal prodemocratic organizations have been seen as its purest manifestations. Bojan Baća draws a distinction between *compliant* and *contentious* postsocialist civil society. *Compliant* civil society is in tune with the top-down postsocialist transition with its "formal, institutional and routinized ways of settling disputes"; *contentious* civil society describes unaccounted-for civic action—from infrapolitical action with indirect political consequences, to horizontal democratic organizing that disputes the legitimacy of institutions, to illegal endeavors in the informal economy as part of the struggle for survival. The contentious action approach looks for patterns at the level of practice, often based in direct action, ways that address nonresponsive state structures and problems in daily life. See Bojan Baća, "Practice Theory and Postsocialist Civil Society: Toward a New Analytical Framework," *International Political Sociology* (September 2021), https://doi.org/10.1093/ips/olab021.

41. Timotijević, "Joint Action Roof Over Head"; Vilenica, Mentus, and Ristić, "Struggles for Care Infrastructures in Serbia: The Pandemic, Dispossessed Care, and Housing."

commoning could be described as a permanent or temporary practice that connects material infrastructure (shelter, water, sewage, roads, etc.), knowledge production, affects, care, and food distribution networks, to preserve the existing housing infrastructure or create new ones at the margins.[42] Tenants, their allies and accomplices, as well as material infrastructures, are among the potential actors in housing commoning. Housing commoning is more than a temporary fix intended to fill gaps left by an inefficient welfare system. It also includes militant political acts that show the failure of the system to deal with the permanent housing crisis. Although the state tolerates some aspects of self-care and solidarity to fill the gaps it has created, its repressive apparatus does not hesitate to criminalize acts directly intervening in its practice of "transitional" business as usual that favors the right to property over the right to a home.

In my research and activist practice, I've come to identify two types of contentious practice that include commoning in housing struggles in Serbia: *activist housing commoning* and *housing commoning in liminality*. They are sometimes tactically intertwined. To local activists, decision makers and academics, the first counts as social movement, struggle, protest, "heroic resistance," and/or commoning. The second does not. Activist housing commoning takes place where middle-class activists provide support to those subjected to housing dispossession and precarity, work towards policy changes, and build cooperative housing alternatives.

The anti-eviction movement that emerged in 2017 in reaction to an eviction epidemic that started with the privatization of the bailiff protocol is a good example. It consisted of middle-class, left-oriented activists working together to help people resist eviction from their homes. This movement had the effect of politicizing the unjust systemic changes in the housing sector and increased anti-bailiff sentiment, bringing temporary halts to eviction through direct action as well as legal action such as the constitutional review initiative against the Law on Enforcement and Security. Another example is the movement addressing the issue of forced displacement by the multinational corporation Rio Tinto by organizing protests alongside people in nearby villages who refuse to sell their homes and land. Reacting to the government's attempt to introduce changes in the law for land expropriation that would help Rio Tinto take over the land it desires, this movement has gathered hundreds of thousands of people from

---

42. Dombroski, Diprose, and Boles, "Can the Commons be Temporary?"

left, liberal, and right-wing provenances—vaxxers and anti-vaxxers alike—at road blockades across Serbia. In these examples, the self-organization of local people is supported by existing environmental and left-wing organizations in a time of crisis while the biggest burden remains with the people on the ground. Green and left actors with parliamentary ambitions have also used their participation in these movements as symbolic capital to form new political parties and political alliances. These movement formations are usually locally embodied but transnationally connected, with the (un)intended effect of a hierarchical division between "victims" who risk everything and activists who heroically stand in their defense who may risk going to jail or being fined. Housing commons activists have also made efforts to overcome generalized housing precarity via the research and development of cooperative housing models that could offer affordable alternatives to the unaffordable housing market in the future.[43] Although activists have succeeded in changing the legal framework to recognize housing cooperatives, many procedural, legal, and financial obstacles continue to prevent this model from coming to life.

In contrast, commoning in liminality takes place in illegalized, informalized, underground, irregular, impermanent, or temporary spaces defined by negation.[44] According to official estimates in 2015, there were 580 self-organized settlements in the country, inhabited mostly by Roma. The number of self-organized settlements made by migrants from Asia and African countries is constantly changing due to the hostility of the environment. In these liminal spaces a place is made in seemingly uninhabitable conditions where "the labor is not merely a constellation of survivalist strategies but rather a formation of logics and practices that make something out of nothing—a mode of dwelling and hustling that form alongside and through diverse forms of breakdown."[45] These liminal spaces—slums, Roma mahalas, squats of the urban poor, and self-organized settlements of migrants—can be seen as related to the colonial legacy of

---

43. Ana Vilenica, Ana Džokic, and Marc Neelen, "Affordable Housing in Your Lifetime?" in *The Social Production of Architecture—Politics, Values and Actions in Contemporary Practice*, ed. Doina Petrescu and Kim Trogal (London: Routledge, 2017): 245–257.

44. Michele Lancione and AbdouMaliq Simone, "Dwelling in Liminalities, Thinking beyond Inhabitation," *Environment and Planning D: Society and Space* 39, no. 6 (July 2021): 969–975; Tatiana A. Thieme, "Beyond Repair: Staying with Breakdown at the Interstices," *Environment and Planning D: Society and Space* 39, no. 6 (July 2021): 1092–1110.

45. Thieme, "Beyond Repair."

weaving informality as a problem.[46] Very often, institutions and activists tend to approach this way of life as mere survival outside the political, failing to look at housing beyond its characteristic as a physical resource. S M Waliuzzaman looks at slum dwellers as a "heterogeneous group of commoners who come together to transform a piece of land into a functional living space."[47] In his opinion, it is not a lack of material resources that limits the ability of commoners to improve living conditions—it is rather illegalization that is the obstacle. The constant threat of eviction due to illegal status of such housing solutions makes people reluctant to invest time and resources in repairs and improve living conditions. Legislation also makes these spaces vulnerable to right-wing racist attacks justified by the belief that these people don't belong there. On the other hand, constant institutional victimization of dwellers of liminal spaces produces internal divides among people. State and NGO humanitarian aid is mostly organized according to specific dividing lines that categorize people into vulnerable groups, which often results in turning people against one another on the bases of nationality, ethnicity, and immigration status. For instance, those who consider themselves native to a particular settlement are often unwelcoming to neighbors with the status of "internally displaced" who are more likely to receive support from NGOs.

In recent times, the direct action approach of activists has opened up a new potentiality for commoning by connecting activists to people in struggle on their doorstep. Increasing housing precarity has motivated activists to look for housing alternatives based on commons principles inspired mostly by examples from Western European countries, such as the Netherlands or Germany, where informal settlements are less significant and social benefits are more robust. These are models in which housing for the urban poor rarely finds a place. Unfortunately, valuable lessons to be learned from commoning in liminality are to a large extent ignored. This is due to an approach that tries to find solutions within imposed Westernized legal frameworks and with reference to "good practices" that have been developed in very different circumstances. To open up to local lessons, activists would need to move from understanding homes as a mere shelter towards an understanding based on the complex reproduction of life that

---

46. S M Waliuzzaman, *A Commons Perspective on Urban Informal Settlements: A Study of Kalyanpur slum in Dhaka, Bangladesh*, PhD dissertation, School of Earth and Environment, University of Canterbury, Auckland, New Zealand (October 2020).

47. Waliuzzaman, *A Commons Perspective on Urban Informal Settlements*, 1.

takes place in and around homes and persists despite imposed precarity and humanitarian divisions. This approach could potentially also contribute to supporting the autonomous political capacity of poor and working-class people instead of reproducing a "white savior" attitude and practice.

Activist commoning projects in Serbia can create and sustain the conditions of possibility required for nurturing commoner subjectivities and countering dominant forms of housing, urban development, and planning. They also provide fertile ground for learning about how to common better. Commoning is a constant struggle between temporary and long-term achievements that have potential to normalize practices of commoning for a wider range of people and institutions. It is not a straightforward practice with clear borders but a messy one dependent on its historical and material circumstances and historical configurations of imagining society in common. Understanding and enacting the local history of housing commoning and struggle evolves in a dialectical way. This is a practice of trying while admitting we are not there yet. To produce this new dialectic of commons and commoning we must address the idealization of certain elements. We can improve upon our approach, learning not only from good practices but from mistakes as well. By developing practices of radical observation, radical self-criticism, and radical humility we can get over the fear of not knowing all the answers.

Chapter 2

FROM THE NEOLIBERAL CITY TO DISASTER CAPITALISM, FROM COMMONS TO "UNENCLOSURE"

Anthony Iles

> London is a razor, an inflamed calm has settled, we're trapped outside
> on its rim. . . . [It's] hard to concentrate what with all the police raids,
> the punishment beatings, the retaliatory fires. It'd be too much to say the
> city's geometry has changed, but it's getting into some fairly wild buck-
> ling. It's gained in dimension, certain things are impossible to recognise,
> others are all too clear.
> —Sean Bonney, "Letter on Silence: Tuesday, August 30, 2011"

Sean Bonney's poem offers us a terrifying vision of the city in which its very
form is being broken and reshaped by the forces bearing upon it. "We"
are relegated to the periphery, "we're trapped outside on its rim." From
this position of marginality, recognition is proving difficult, our familiar
coordinates are becoming estranged to us, yet this perpetual marginality
and vulnerability is a common experience. This text then is an attempt to
restore historicity and the potential for change to this common experience
of psychic and social estrangement, physical and social displacement, from
the cities in which we live.

The experience of the commons, and what prevents it, is very much a
man-made process in London and the UK. Gentrification was first identified and named by London-based urban geographer Ruth Glass, and

culture-led regeneration—a form of state-led urban development—was pioneered in Tony Blair's 1990s Britain and aggressively exported by elements of his policy team worldwide.[1] While widely criticized, the creative city model has far from completely collapsed.[2] However, practical and theoretical opposition to it has become a substantial force, and as I argue here, in this process art has been made both the alibi and internal antagonist of urban redevelopment projects. Art has also become a key placeholder for the commons, and discourses of the commons have increasingly been taken up within the arts as well as in activism globally.[3]

In this chapter, I locate the unfolding concept and reality of the commons in the UK through both specific historical legacies of anticapitalist theory and practice as well as more vague and pluralistic contemporary significations. Using the concept of commons, I analyze recent shifts in the language used to describe state-led or developer-led urban transformation projects in the UK. I trace the search for a regained sense of agency in the urban environment through culture, by returning to the looser and historically aleatory concept of the "commons" as holding open an arena of struggle and agency—of accessible everyday practices—in the face of excessive capitalizations of space, language, and subjectivity.

This chapter presents some tools which have been used to approach the imbrication of capital, space, and class in capitalist urban development. Developing connections between concepts and practices, I conclude my contribution with a glossary of concepts on commons. The cauldron for the development of these concepts has been the postwar development of cities in the UK and US, from which the contribution of urban geographers and others have derived the understandings then subsequently applied to related global processes and situations. The basis for these concepts and their insights in turn relates to Marxian and historical debates about the structuring of rural and urban development, origins of capitalism and the working class, philosophy of history, and

---

1. See Ruth Glass, "Introduction: Aspects of Change," in *London: Aspects of Change* (London: MacGibbon & Kee, 1964); James Heartfield, "Creative London," *Mute*, October 6, 2007, https://www.metamute.org/editorial/articles/creative-london.

2. See *The Creative City in Ruins*, Mute 2, no. 12 (June 2009), https://www.metamute.org/editorial/magazine/mute-vol-2-no.-12-%E2%88%92-creative-city-ruins; Matteo Pasquinelli, *Animal Spirits: A Bestiary of the Common* (Amsterdam: Institute of Network Cultures, 2008).

3. For a thoughtful exploration of this convergence, see Marina Vishmidt, "All Shall Be Unicorns: About Commons, Aesthetics and Time," *Open* (September 2014), https://online-open.org/all-shall-be-unicorns.

teleology. These debates of the nineteenth and early twentieth centuries implicated a global territory encompassing, at its most ambitious, the entirety of humanity, nature, the planet, and at points, even extraterrestrial territory. It must be acknowledged that the scope of these debates has shrunk along with the shrinking scope for imagination, constrained by the limits implied by capitalist development and the imaginaries it allows for. With the crossing point, as observed by US geographer Mike Davis in 2004, of the threshold of "a watershed in human history," by which "[f]or the first time the urban population of the earth will outnumber the rural," the epoch of rural power, or anticipation of a lever of alternative development, or even power against the power of cities and urban capitalism has fundamentally passed and been lost.[4] These may seem outlying concerns, but I argue that they are fundamental limits structuring intellectual debates, artistic imagination, and spatial practices. I conclude the essay by returning to the looser and historically aleatory concept of the "commons" as holding open an arena of struggle and agency—of accessible everyday practices—in the face of excessive capitalizations of space, language, and subjectivity.

Situating the Commons

My direct experiences with commons has spanned housing myself and others and supporting occupied social centers as part of London's squatting movement; supporting local groups of "marsh users" in their defense of a small area of "Lammas Land" (a surviving commons with associated use rights pertaining to grazing animals, gathering of wood, and water use in Waltham Forest, East London); generating and circulating critical writing about a megaproject carried out under the umbrella of the London 2012 Olympics (which impinged on the historical commons mentioned above as well as purpose-built cooperatively-owned social housing, several travelers' sites, allotments, and other crucial amenities).[5]

---

4. Mike Davis, "Planet of the Slums," *New Left Review* 26 (March–April 2004), https://newleftreview.org/issues/ii26/articles/mike-davis-planet-of-slums.

5. Notably, each of these amenities, prior to their destruction, found aspects of their consistency and coherence in anomaly to dominant property relations or norms of habitation. For a definition of Lammas Land in this context, see Anthony Iles, "Of Lammas Land and Olympic Dreams," *Mute*, January 6, 2007, https://www.metamute.org/editorial/articles/lammas-land-and-olympic-dreams.

This activity was extended in a journalistic and theoretical vein in my role as an editor at *Mute*, critically following the development of discourses and practices of urban regeneration in the UK. The critique of a "digital commons" that developed at *Mute*—whereby enthusiasm for an emergent commons was shown to be based on the invention of new legal norms, as well as the privation and monetization of "free" activity—was also a key site of learning and understanding around the issue of commons both present and historical.[6] Thinking through this conjuncture of the commons as encompassing contestations around urban space, digital media, intellectual property, and copyright has also been developed through my maintenance of an online library of digitized texts by the US autonomist Marxist publishing collective Midnight Notes.[7] Indeed, *Mute* was one of the key sites for developing their concept of the "new enclosures" in the UK, through writing published in the magazine and on the website between the late 1990s and early 2000s.[8]

Another route into discussions of the commons at *Mute* was via the long tradition of "history from below,"[9] its concentration and politicization by the postwar New Left (E.P. Thompson, Dorothy Thompson, A.L. Morton, Christopher Hill, Raphael Samuel, and many others), and the connections between their studies of historical enclosure in the UK and the activities of the peace movement in the 1950s through the late 1980s.[10]

---

6. A key special issue being *Underneath The Knowledge Commons*, *Mute* 2, no. 1 (December 2005), https://www.metamute.org/editorial/magazine/mute-vol-2-no.-1-%E2%88%92 -underneath-knowledge-commons.

7. Anthony Iles, "Midnight Notes Digitized," Memory of the World Library (2015), https:// www.memoryoftheworld.org/blog/2015/05/27/repertorium_midnight_notes_digitized/.

8. An excellent example of the relation between new enclosures and disaster capitalism is Benedict Seymour's prescient essay on the man-made disaster following Hurricane Katrina, see "Drowning by Numbers: The Non-Reproduction of New Orleans," *Mute* (December 2006), https://www.metamute.org/editorial/articles/drowning-numbers-non-re-production-new-orleans. Notably, an earlier uptake of Midnight Notes' concepts of the commons and new enclosures in relationship to housing, class, land, and gentrification struggles in the UK took place at the end of the 1980s. See the anthology *No Reservations: Housing, Space and Class Struggle* (London: News From Everywhere, 1989), reviewed in Red Menace, *The Red Menace* 4 (September/October 1989), https://libcom.org/library/ help-economy-sleep-streets-red-menace.

9. For a survey, see Anthony Iles and Tom Roberts, *All Knees and Elbows of Susceptibility and Refusal: Reading History from Below* (Glasgow and London: The Strickland Distribution, Transmission Gallery, and Mute Books, 2002), https://archive.leftove.rs/documents/AIWD/.

10. The famous Women's Peace Camp occupied land beside a joint US-UK military airbase at Greenham Common by exploiting surviving common law protecting continuous rights to access to common land. Many military, nuclear power, and other highly secure state assets are situated on common land in the UK. See Frances Reed, *On Common Ground* (London: Working Press, 1991).

Many writers associated with *Mute* picked up on the class-oriented and alter-globalist writing of the Midnight Notes Collective, and through that the work of the New Left historians (among whom Peter Linebaugh, as a former student of the Thompsons, and member of both the Warwick Crime Group and Midnight Notes, is one important mediating figure; Silvia Federici, with her strong connections to Italian autonomist Marxism and the global feminist movement, is another). Writers contributing to *Mute* then sought to use the concept of enclosure to bridge and correct a certain smoothness around commons as a metaphor as it was being used then—in the late 1990s to early 2000s—by Italian Marxists (Paolo Virno, Antonio Negri, and others), social movements oriented towards the alter-globalization movement, and rapidly being ported into the realm of digital rights and privacy.[11]

Commons discourse began to reveal problematic facets during this period because, as we learned during the intensive privatizations in the UK of the 1990s and 2000s, in the face of the necessary defense of a concrete social resource: a swimming pool, a local library, a local advice center. . . a looser, positive discourse of commons can lead us to understand that the disciplinary encoding of local institutions is best left behind for something lighter on its feet, more mutable—supposedly more open to transformation by its users, more temporary, etc. But lurking behind these loose forms are indeed harder forms of ownership, law, and cryptohierarchy (hierarchical organizations which dissimulate as nonhierarchical forms). Similarly, in feminist discussions, criticism of the ways in which women generally are treated as a 'commons'—a free resource to be exploited—by capital and patriarchal culture generally, has rightly put in question assumptions of the positivity of 'natural' roles and that which is thought to be *outside* of capital's grasp. Now that the commons has become a global concept used critically by social movements as well as uncritically and vaguely by all sorts of other actors and formations, I hope to contribute to these debates, renewing the commons as a critical concept by positioning it in relation to other radical concepts and political positions. Throughout these experiences I have attempted to communicate, as I continue to do here, a conception of

---

11. For example, see Gregor Claude, "Goatherds in Pinstripes," in *Mute* 1, no. 23 (March 2002), https://www.metamute.org/editorial/articles/goatherds-pinstripes; Peter Linebaugh, "Charters of Liberty in Black Face and White Face: Race, Slavery and the Commons," *Mute* 2, no. 2 (November 2005), https://www.metamute.org/editorial/articles/charters-liberty-black-face-and-white-face-race-slavery-and-commons.

commons which ensures it is living and antagonistic, and not idealized or affirmative.[12]

Art's Changing Relationship to the Neoliberal City

Under neoliberalism, the commodification of space relentlessly intensifies, bursting through previous barriers, augmenting time and seemingly unlimited (proportional and quantitative) expansions of rent. Space seems to eat itself and every activity occupying it is forced to move aside for something more profitable, finally standing empty as the container of a purely speculative ingot of its own promise of future rent. Limits to profit and to expansion established by prior legal norms—e.g., the right to housing, management of certain key infrastructural sectors by the state, fire, and health regulations—become contested, flexible, financialized, deregulated, or simply liquidated.

Finance is now integral to the way that productive capitalism operates, notably with major producers of real goods (e.g., cars) accruing a significant portion of their profits from using their workers' pensions as speculative capital deployed on open markets and in the sphere of circulation. Crucially too, where property and urbanization have been safe havens during crises of overaccumulation, today, with finance in a leading and constitutive role, urbanization is a crucial and constant mediator within the new shape of capital accumulation.[13]

London as a city is more financialized than ever, and its image, both swanky and multicultural, is the paradigm for other global cities increasingly competing to attract the same financial services and high net-worth individuals. This emerging vision (part projection, part reality) suggests that there is no real city beneath the parasitical suction mechanisms of finance, but rather that finance is the fabric, force, and substance flowing between the city's bricks and surfaces. With the enormous public bailouts of 2008 this has become the de facto truth. The entire economy is ransomed to the fortunes of finance, which provides higher returns than production,

---

12. Iles, "'Of Lammas Land and Olympic Dreams.'"

13. "'Real property' (along with construction) is no longer a secondary form of circulation, no longer the auxiliary and balanced branch of industry and financial capitalism that it once was. Instead, it has a leading role, albeit in an uneven way, for its significance is liable to vary according to country, time or circumstance." Henri Lefebvre, quoted in Louis Moreno, "The urban process under financialized capitalism," *City* 18, no. 3 (June 2014): 244–268.

making production increasingly impossible. The consequences are the continuing deindustrialization of sites of production, the imbrication of culture in the commodification of space, and an increasing industrialization of service work, including art.

Responding to this climate, in 2007–2008 Josephine Berry and I began work on *No Room to Move*, a book surveying the history of the entwinement of public art and urban regeneration in the UK during the postwar period to reevaluate the consequences of their convergence at the moment of a global financial crisis following the collapse of a speculative housing bubble.[14] Preceding this crash, many commentators had remarked on the apparent loss of autonomy for the arts in situations where, on the one hand, artists participating in urban regeneration projects seemed liable to submit to the instrumentalizing imperatives of speculative development, while on the other hand, artists' spatial resources were threatened by gentrification and they tended to be displaced in almost equal measure as other low-income inhabitants residing in the path of such projects. Nonetheless, we held on to several linked modes of autonomy developed by artists facing these pressures. At that time, we wrote:

> It seems future generations of artists will continue to face the contradictory bind of being both beneficiaries and losers in the path of capital's movement of creative destruction (each time on reconfigured terms and conditions). And as art and artists have become more integral to contemporary urbanism, they have also become increasingly astute critics. Yet moments when artists directly resist development and gentrification directly have been relatively rare. Art works more often mount an aesthetic resistance or, as Jacques Rancière would say, a 'redistribution of the sensible.' Critical art in urban settings survives development's horrors, maintaining a tension with the context of its production and, in the best cases, amplifying them. Rather than writing off art altogether as either 'for or against' regeneration, should we not rather consider aesthetic experiments in terms of tensions they establish with their contexts and the forces which attempt to direct them?[15]

---

14. See *Living in a Bubble: Credit, Debt & Crisis, Mute* 2, no. 6 (September 2007), https://www.metamute.org/editorial/magazine/mute-vol-2-no.-6-%E2%88%92- living-bubble-credit-debt-crisis.

15. Josephine Berry Slater and Anthony Iles, *No Room to Move: Radical Art and the Regenerate City* (London: Mute Books, 2010), 23.

In more recent work, Josephine Berry and I further develop the framework established in *No Room to Move* by which we understood art developing both in relation to and distinction from capitalism's "spatial fixes."[16] This has meant deepening our inquiry into the relationships between financialization and urbanism, and in order to do that, we returned to the original work of Marxists exploring the evolving relationships of space to capital over the nineteenth, twentieth, and twenty-first centuries.

Ends of Regeneration

The first wave of culture-led regeneration took place as the Conservative government's response to the widespread urban riots of 1981. In 1984 and 1985, "Garden Festivals" were held in five cities which had been tainted by class violence during the riots. Under a rhetoric of job creation and the smokescreen of culture, the festivals facilitated the assembling of large parcels of derelict and highly polluted industrial sites for their remediation and then sale to large developers at discount rates after the show left town. Though widely mocked and hardly lucrative for the developers, it nonetheless achieved a substantial transfer of wealth from the public purse to the private sphere, establishing a model for the direct intervention of the state in forcing gentrification through the mediation of culture. This model would be taken up with a vengeance by the Labour government following Thatcher. The first large-scale regeneration project in the UK was the London Docklands—a former system of docks in East London—that would become the city's second financial center. In this historically working-class district, regeneration began with a coordinated effort to provide artist studios, famously including the Young British Artists, with Damien Hirst becoming a kind of broker between the state and real estate developers. What was previously informal and self-organized—artists and musicians accessing vacant industrial space free or for low rent—became incorporated into a premeditated entrepreneurial scheme driven and coordinated by a unity of private and state interests. Between 1981–1994, the Docklands received an estimated £390 million in public funding to build an entirely private business zone surrounded

---

16. See Josephine Berry and Anthony Iles, "The Exploitation of Isolation: Urban Development and the Artist's Studio," in Ana Vilenica, ed., *Radical Housing: Art, Struggle, Care* (Amsterdam: Institute of Network Cultures, 2021).

by water and protected by private security and bylaws controlling normal access rights.[17]

After its election victory in 1997, the New Labour government announced its agenda of "Urban Renaissance." Targeting forty-two inner-city areas characterized by large-scale, local authority-built housing estates in a New Deal for Communities, a national program of "improvement" was implemented over the next decade.[18] The results were everywhere the same—estate demolitions, privatization of local services, welfare reform, and criminalization of youth—altogether resulting in widespread displacement of working-class communities. To accompany this process, a whole mini-industry of commissioning services, consultants, brand agencies, public artists, landscape and lighting designers grew around the regeneration gravy train. Reshaping the material fabric of the city and its class relations, "regeneration" sought to smooth the passage of capital investment, pool liquidity, and create ease of access to state funds and resources in a form of "capitalist commoning."

As part of the same movement, disinvestment (by restricting funds to local government) or divestment (by forcing local government to sell off public assets) occurred as publicly owned resources were sold off or broken up to suit the interests of this movement of privatization. This could take the form of direct transfer of wealth to the private sphere—a sell off, land grab, or theft—or the mechanism of debt may be used to bind the state into a relationship of dependency upon the private interests of the market. Meanwhile, new antisocial behavior legislation and a para-legal apparatus punished recalcitrance or noncompliance with the new regimes of the deregulated labor market being put in place.[19] By the late 1990s and 2000s, London's regeneration was rapidly becoming merely a passing phase. National urban programs began to wane and sources of funding dried up. With this, art increasingly became a "vanishing mediator." With the intense inflation of the housing bubble and the shifting balance of power between developers and the local state, councils have become dependent on developers to deliver local services, transportation links, and other amenities.

---

17. See "About LDCC–A Brief Overview," http://www.lddc-history.org.uk/lddcachieve/.

18. Gerard Lemos, "Forgotten No Longer," *The Guardian*, September 29, 1999, https://www.theguardian.com/society/1999/sep/29/regeneration.guardiansocietysupplement.

19. Sean Creaney and Roger Hopkins-Burke, "A 'new' response to anti-social behaviour: early reflections on the Anti-Social Behaviour, Crime and Policing Act 2014," *Safer Communities* 13, no. 4 (2015): 161–170.

Nonetheless, the formula was addictive and many councils have continued to pursue the agenda set in the New Labour years. A sort of zombie regeneration or low-budget ethical gentrification persists.

Post-financial crisis, post-lockdown, and post-Brexit, several local councils in London have recently found themselves bankrupt or close to bankruptcy. Most emblematically, the very populous borough of Croydon in South London, who cut social services and accumulated debt and other liabilities while attempting to facilitate the redevelopment of a major shopping center.[20] As implied by the trajectory plotted by Peter Roberts in his "Table of the Evolution of Urban Regeneration" (2000), state-led regeneration schemes have increasingly given way to raw appropriation of resources based on which certain entities have the most money and least social responsibilities. These inevitably turn out to be private rather than state actors.[21] Although London councils could position themselves to borrow sufficient money to build on a small to medium scale to address their inhabitants' housing needs, generally they are far too liable to risk, and more strongly obligated to observe building, health, and safety standards. Private entities have rapidly developed complex means perfectly suited to the UK's deregulated and financialized business environment to evade legal and fiscal liabilities. The local state simply cannot compete in the current environment, and therefore fewer large-scale regeneration schemes are launched by councils. Councils find their ability to contribute any coherent urban plan or exercise much control over speculative schemes occurring in their territory more limited now than at any point in the past. Their powers seem constrained either to working to divest from and demolish local authority-built housing to clear them for denser schemes based on primarily private sales, or to offset what has been privatized and destroyed by supporting community project grants, pocket parks, pedestrianizing streets, or providing cycle lanes. Yet these minor environmental improvements will not do anything to bring back well-built affordable housing and instead tend to increase the value and thus price of the surrounding privately-owned housing.

---

20. Inside Croydon, "Croydon in crisis: BBC says at least five councils could go bust," *Inside Croydon*, June 25, 2022, https://insidecroydon.com/2020/06/25/croydon-in-crisis-bbc-says-at-least-five-councils-could-go-bust/.

21. Peter Roberts, "Table of the Evolution of Urban Regeneration," in *Urban Regeneration: A Handbook*, ed. Peter Roberts and Hugh Sykes (London, Thousand Oaks, New Delhi: Sage, 2000), 14.

At this moment, the collapse of art's autonomy has become ever more frequently imbricated with the threat to the autonomy of certain social resources. With the rapid privatization and loss of state-supported public culture (itself always questionably patriarchal, exclusive, and exclusionary), art has found sympathy with fragments of "common sense" residing in everyday forms and spaces. Yet where art has lent its special exceptionality to the defense of social resources, undermines exactly the possibility of those resources' universality. Just as David Harvey recognized the role of art within the new forms of rent-seeking urbanism as providing uniqueness and authenticity through the individual, but inherently social, pursuit of particularity, the practical dangers of art affirming the particularity of a commons is that this simply attracts and provides new pathways for the rent-seeking bulldozers. I would argue, rather, the other side of art's "common sense" should be thought of in its propensity to catalyze new forms of critical judgment and negativity. At this phase in the dialectic of capitalist urbanism and art, it is perhaps better to bring art's negativity and particularity to poison the wells of the worst of capital's non-spaces than to draw attention to new resources for it to pillage.

In the following sections I attempt to explore some of the active tendencies and ways I have been thinking through them in the context of London after the financial crisis and during the pandemic, as well as drawing on some examples beyond my immediate local purview.

Developer Driven Art

An earlier stage of creative-led regeneration has been superseded by its reverse: developer-driven art. At the present juncture, much of the activity we charted in our first foray into studying art's role and relation to the neoliberal city has disappeared. The public art bubble that was briefly, and quite spectacularly inflated by the New Labour government (1997–2010), has been rapidly deflating ever since the 2008 financial crisis. More imposing than the Tate Modern, that millennial symbol of Creative Britain, is the rash of glass towers that have grown up around it.[22] This image crystallizes, at the level of the city skyline, suspicions that art's urban appearances within

---

22. A conflagration explored with aplomb by Andrew Harris in an article which for us has both an allegorical significance in terms of London's housing provision and material consequences for art. See Andrew Harris, "Livingstone versus Serota: The High-Rise Battle of Bankside," *The London Journal* 33, no. 3 (2008): 289–299.

the late 1990s and 2000s were always just a vanishing mediator between the old, deindustrialized city and its revalorization as a city of financial speculation. Where the Tate Modern symbolized the then-emerging triumphant compact between art and finance at the millennium,[23] London's oldest financial district is now (we don't know yet for how long) a ghost town and the Tate is increasingly a hotbed of labor unrest. As direct funding for varied species of public art within cultural regeneration schemes has fallen away in the post-crisis period, accompanied by ad hoc suspensions of developers' obligations outside the narrow drive to generate profit (e.g., the relaxing of Section 106 contributions and drastic reduction of affordable housing quotients), art's use in promoting inner cities as ripe for investment has been superseded by a developer land grab which, for the most part, only requires the veneer of creativity. This change of tack has coincided with a slashing of central government and local authority funding for art and culture and a retreat of public commissioning.[24]

We recognize that developer-driven art is an oxymoron, and although something of this nature might exist, it certainly can't any longer be considered art, but rather an assimilation and imitation of its operations. While this situation made such ventures more beholden to private capital it has also pushed forking tendencies in two directions: one in which the developer absorbs some of the delivery functions of the local state, another where developers have dispensed entirely with any semblance of social amelioration and sought to create entirely private enclaves crenellated with appropriately feudal insignia (horses, knights, kings, and weaponry).

One of the key examples I like to cite to illustrate this trajectory is a public sculpture by Peter Dunn in Weavers Fields, Bethnal Green, East London. Dunn is well known for his activist work with Lorraine Leeson against the London Docklands Development Corporation. Dunn's 2003 sculpture indicates not only the mutable values of artists, but also of the constraints under which they make their work. *Weaving Identities* is a vertical welded metal sculpture placed at the center of a public park. Rising from a pedestal decorated by a tiled montage made by schoolchildren, athletic figures soar and rise through

---

23. Anthony Davies and Simon Ford, "Art Capital," *Art Monthly*, no. 213 (February 1998), http://infopool.antipool.org/artcap.htm.

24. David Pilditch writes, "Alarming new figures show council spending on museums, galleries, libraries, and local arts has plunged by more than £390 million since 2011." See Pilditch, "£400m cuts leave museums in crisis," *Daily Express*, January 29, 2019, https://www.express.co.uk/news/uk/1079497/400m-cuts-museums-crisis-libraries-public-fundings.

FIGURE 2.1. *Denys Mitchell, The Knight of the Cnihtengild (1990), beaten bronze and blue crystal, Devonshire Square, Bishopsgate, London. Commissioned by Standard Life Insurance Company. Photo by Anthony Iles.*

the air only to reach an apex at which there are four CCTV cameras scouring quadrants of the park. Masquerading as benign community art celebrating local athleticism, it is in fact a security device. This, along with Anish Kapoor's *ArcelorMittal Orbit* (2012) at the London Olympic site, for me, exemplifies the myriad ways London's current direction of development kills what it loves, destroying diversity in the name of diversity, proclaiming wildly that it wants art and creativity but making of it an offensive antisocial weapon.[25]

---

25. Kapoor's sculpture masquerades as "autonomous art" but was in fact bound by an initial condition set by its patron, Arcelor Mittal, an Indian-born global mining tycoon, stipulating that materials from each of his major mining ventures be included in the sculptural form. The second condition, which transformed the sculpture from an object of aesthetic contemplation into a leisure/entertainment facility, was provided by then Mayor of London now former UK Prime Minister, Boris Johnson, who insisted the sculpture provide a viewing platform and slide for visitors to the Olympic Park. See Forensic Architecture, "A Memorial in Exile," *Mute*, June 28, 2012, https://www.metamute.org/community/your-posts/memorial-exile.

FIGURE 2.2. *Peter Dunn (Art of Change),* Weaving Identities *(2003), cast stainless steel, Weavers Fields, Bethnal Green, London. Commissioned by LB Tower Hamlets. Photo by Anthony Iles.*

In the current developer's toolkit, we find the absorption of practices developed through contemporary art, but also adjacent art forms: theater, literature, dance, which have equally extended themselves into the "expanded field" of site-specific and noninstitutional social practice. Here we find a logic of participatory commoning, initially configured to break down the rigid encoding of aesthetic experience by the institutions of art, deployed anew to offset, mask, and moderate the social antagonisms which are the inevitable outcome of processes of displacement and the upwards transfer of wealth and resources. We find forms of history and poetic writing attuned to placemaking processes, where place has effectively been erased, because something unowned, available, and accessible has since become closely guarded property.[26] London developers now provide a litany of pseudo-embedded practices, from the establishment of pop-up

---

26. See Anna Minton, "What Kind of World are We Building? The Privatisation of Public Space," RICS (March 2006), https://docs.wixstatic.com/ugd/e87dab_c893a52a18624acdb-94472869d942a09.pdf.

community gardens and bicycle workshops to storytelling, oral history projects, festivals and fun days, in order to ease and mask the shock of the violent acquisition of space, destruction of community resources, and disempowerment of existing communities. Yet, within this, it is not only that one community is being displaced for another. Just as frequently, and muddying clarity over the process, it is individual subjects who are subject to transformation at the center of this process. There are winners and losers; those forced to strive in new conditions and those displaced and relegated to marginality or exile.

Art Becomes Service Work

One of the sites where this transformation of art has taken place in the UK is around the expansion of service work into the field of culture. Not only, as critics such as Claire Bishop have observed, is it the form of art most frequently staged at the Tate's new temple, one of socially engaged participation, which celebrates "self-sufficient consumerism" and "independen[ce] of any need for welfare," but in practice, the form of art and form of labor supporting its exhibition coincide in a toxic stew of contradictions.[27] Many Tate front of house staff are dependent on benefits because their fluctuating casual hours are so scattered and wages so low. Dependence on (small) benefits to supplement low wages not only forms a second subsidy to the Tate's already generous direct sponsorship by the UK government's Department for Digital, Culture, Media & Sport (DCMS), but it also suggests the deliberate creation of a culture of dependence and superfluity rather than agency. As three hundred-plus Tate workers found out in August 2020, this dependence runs only one way; as soon as the Tate found itself in the red by Summer 2020, after the first lockdown in the UK, their lowest paid staff were summarily sacked. On the one hand, institutions such as the Tate increasingly inculcate docile, conformist visitors, the perfect economic subject: "submissive citizens who respect authority and accept the 'risk' and responsibility of looking after themselves in the face of diminished public services."[28] On the other hand, it has industrialized cultural work, pushing wages low and output high, standardizing what was previously skilled

---

27. Claire Bishop, *Artificial Hells: Participatory Art and the Politics of Spectatorship* (London and New York: Verso, 2014), 13.
28. Bishop, *Artificial Hells*, 14.

work, and bringing it closer to the other forms of service work expanding in London to cater to an increasingly wealthy elite who work in close proximity to the financial sector.

Where these two figures of the conformist culture participant and precarious worker coincide in one subject is in the previously burgeoning, but perhaps now passing, phenomenon of property guardianship.[29] Property guardians are essentially workers who protect empty properties awaiting development yet pay a fee for the privilege. Their contracts can last weeks, months, or years. These are unlike any other tenancy contracts (in reality, more like temporary licenses) offered in the UK and ensure very few rights to their signatories.[30] Property guardians are often bohemians or creatives looking for rough big spaces and low rents. In this arrangement, the 24-hour security guard now pays rent for the opportunity only to be displaced with two weeks' notice. However, even amidst this already topsy turvy picture, further directions of development can be gleaned. In 2011, social entrepreneur and former squatter Katharine Hibbert developed a form of "socially responsible property guardianship."[31] This business, known as Dot Dot Dot, claims social credibility by encouraging property guardians not only to pay for the privilege of occupying real estate developers' empty properties but also to carry out voluntary work in the local area. From the Dot Dot Dot company, it was a short leap to arts organization Bow Arts, then situated in the maelstrom of one of the most intensive programs of privatization of social housing in East London, to broker this form of live/work tenure to artists as a replacement for more traditional forms of subsidized studio provision.[32] Where many artists took advantage of the earlier informal schemes because of the high cost of studio and living space in London, these new schemes not only demand rent, but tangible participation in the urban redevelopment process. Since the withering of regeneration schemes directed at the national level, new agencies are exploiting the

---

29. For an excellent overview, based on research conducted in London from 2016 to 2018, see Ana Vilenica, "The Doomed Pursuit of Dignity: Artists as Property Guardians in and Against Artwashing," *AM Journal* 25 (2021): 185–196.

30. "PGs are not paid for their guardian services, they have to pay a fee (not rent), in order to temporarily use the space, which is often dilapidated and unsuitable for housing, but usually larger and located centrally. The temporary licenses on the bases of which the property guardians use the space can be terminated at 2 weeks' notice, which is the major drawback of this kind of arrangement." See Vilenica, "The Doomed Pursuit of Dignity," 188.

31. See "Our history" on the Dot Dot Dot website, https://dotdotdotproperty.com/about/.

32. See Bow Arts, https://bowarts.org/.

déclassé image of artists in modernity: artists' discomfort, exceptionality, bohemianism, and poverty are instrumentalized within these schemes to make of them "embedded agent[s] of regeneration."[33] Socially responsible property guardians then conform to the principles of "social participation" developed above, in an environment which is conditional upon their exceptional status and compliance, policed on every side by forms of coercive rent extraction.

If the property guardian is the exemplary precarious, though socially responsible subject, the pop-up or "meanwhile space" is the place as project, attuned perfectly to hover between commodity and common until its value can be realized as profit. Viewed retrospectively, after the cycle beginning with the financial crisis of 2007–2008, the pop-up was a *moment* in these former places' violent transition onto the open market. Striking here is how it is now the council flat, residential estate, and community hall that has become newly designated as a (temporary) site of studio production or artistic intervention.[34] In the same way that industrial spaces were planned out of the city in the 1960s, curtailing their actual utility, financialized urban development's need for new sites of value extraction unevenly inflicts long-term obsolescence on entire communities and their homes, producing only short-lived opportunities for artists. This constitutes a total inversion of avant-garde modernism's dreams of master planning the city, with artists no longer employed as visionaries but rather encouraged to pick over the bones of social housing provision.

The "house," whether in the sculptural form of the evacuated single-terraced British *House* (Rachel Whiteread, 1993), or the housing estate maps refined through painterly abstraction as *Estate Maps* (Keith Coventry, 1991–1995), or more antagonistically and expressively in Inventory's *Estate Map* (1999), became a central motif of art in the UK at a moment when the model of habitation seemed simultaneously connected to geopolitical change, reflective of the waning of artistic and architectural modernism, and a microcosm of wider social antagonisms. If in the 1990s houses in art were ciphers for a mourning of the past or for socialism, the late-2000s placement of artists in former local authority housing would produce

33. Richard Whitby, "Angels, The Phoenix, Bats, Battery Hens and Vultures –The Bow Arts Trust Live/Work Scheme" (np, 2011), https://www.academia.edu/2560146/Angels_The_Phoenix_Bats_Battery_Hens_and_ Vultures_The_Bow_Arts_Trust_Live_Work_Scheme.

34. Bow Arts live/work scheme at the monolithic local authority housing estate Thamesmead is a key example, see https://bowarts.org/studios/lakeside-centre-thamesmead.

critical meditations on the image of the house and the social question of housing (Jessie Brennan, 2015–ongoing; Laura Oldfield Ford, 2008–ongoing; Alex Frost, 2014–2015), as well as some very public moments of hubris as artistic ambition met with raw discontent over housing poverty and the mistreatment of tenants facing "estate regeneration."[35] From the association of progress with the past to the insight that progress is no longer possible, we are now forced to inhabit the very processes which make progress impossible. The small number of artists who revolted against these grotesque conditions from inside them—to expose exactly how they were neither natural nor inevitable—were making and inventing politics where the political had been effaced as much as a critical art where a feebler sibling was intended to emerge. In the cramped space between the diminishing stock of social housing and rising culture of property speculation, such critiques were necessarily issued "not with any critical distance but rather from a conflicted and implicated position."[36] Looking back to 2009 from the present, this is one of the few perspectives from which housing privatization, art, space, and property enter into a fully antagonistic and dynamic entanglement by which art's critical relationship to society is exercised and developed.

In this context, "decorative art"—that is, art which does not insist on negativity vis-à-vis the forces it comes into contact with—becomes a vehicle of the reactive individualizing struggle for distinction; that is, taste, or worse: simple distraction from the violent processes of dispossession and displacement which urban regeneration projects mask. Where art is deployed as a vehicle for particularity in this way, as the means of offsetting the blandness of contemporary urban products, it bypasses its potential universality, jettisoning its critical capacities. Marcus Coates' *Vision Quest: A Ritual for Elephant & Castle* (2015) falls between these two, the Scylla and Charybdis of the contemporary artist in urban regeneration's *Odyssey*. Playing out a staple colonial plotline of a "rogue consultant" "going native" against the backdrop of destruction of the Heygate Estate and running down of the Elephant & Castle shopping center, the film absorbs the latent energies and conflicts of the Elephant area and concentrates only to obscure them (e.g., deflecting attention from substantive tenant organizing) and

---

35. Christopher Jones, "Pyramid Dead," *Mute,* April 17, 2014, https://www.metamute.org/editorial/articles/pyramid-dead-artangel-history.

36. Alex Frost, "Property Guardian," at Flat Time House, June 5–August 2, 2015.

purge itself of this compounded suffering as enjoyment and celebrity becoming. Where art is celebrated as wildly subjective, this view forecloses art's inherent objectivity, its factual social existence as both part of and antagonist to what exists. Where art is posed as compensation for subjectivity canceled elsewhere, it participates in the emptying out and banalization of contemporary life by which life is presented as a sequence of choices, likes and dislikes, without ever offering the freedom not to choose, or indeed, to choose freedom.

Looking to the US, Theaster Gates' practice has successfully fused previously disparate coordinates of modernist formalism. He combines the geometric, abstract, craft, material innovation, "primitive," and salvage with the emergent figure of the artist as social entrepreneur and conduit of capital into previously exceptional territories of "zoned disinvestment," such as African American neighborhoods in Chicago. Artists at the head of cultural regeneration appear at the point of greatest need and difficulty, while at smoother, more central sites art appears precisely to introduce roughness, granularity, or simply a sense of place into sites which otherwise would resemble a 3D digital rendering. The idea that artists should control their conditions of work as directly as possible is not in question here, what is questionable is the individual and exceptional distribution of the entrepreneurial models of "worker control" and the private-public capital partnerships they presuppose.[37]

There are various entry points for artists and art workers into this scene, roles span from technician, arts administrator, bottom-feeding service provider (e.g., via a competition to submit a proposal for a public artwork as part of a new development), to producer and engineer of the site and the framework of signification around which development takes place.

37. Marina Vishmidt, "Mimesis of the Hardened and Alienated: Social Practice as Business Model," *e-flux journal*, no. 43 (March 2013), https://www.e-flux.com/journal/43/60197/mimesis-of-the-hardened-and-alienated-social-practice-as-business-model/.

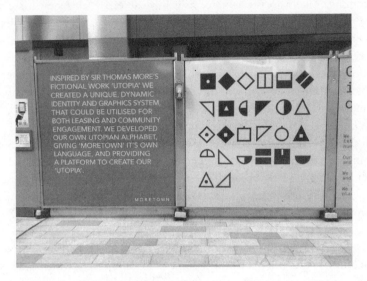

FIGURE 2.3. *Gensler and Resolution Property, Moretown signage and rebranding (c. 2016): A "unique, dynamic identity and graphics system, that could be utilised for both leasing and community engagement." Part of the redevelopment of Thomas More Square, Wapping, London. Photo by Anthony Iles.*

Amidst the hostile environment created by austerity urbanism in the UK, we increasingly stumble over forms of what I am calling "commons dressing" or "commons priming" littering the streets. Where the smallest curbstone is edged with an herb garden and festooned with children's art and a free library, but large low-density blocks built for working people are uncared for, unrepaired (just as their residents are socially scorned), then destroyed. The practice of squatting (officially made illegal for residential properties in 2011) has become structurally marginal with the rising centrality of property to the UK's economy and practically marginal due to the success of property guardianship. While squatting is not simply mappable onto the concept of commons, the constituent power and blurring of property boundaries catalyzed by squatting culture definitely make it proximate to discussions of commons. At this moment, however, resolving housing inequality in the UK demands wide-ranging and structural solutions.[38]

---

38. The inaccessibility of squatting and its inapplicability to many people's housing needs are key reasons why a new generation of housing activists have thrown their weight behind building a mass movement around developing class power and overturning abysmal conditions in the rental sector. For one expression of this, see the London Renters Union, https://londonrentersunion.org/ and another is Living Rent, https://www.livingrent.org/.

Nostalgia for squatting in this context contributes to the operative myopia which has taken hold, denigrating big solutions to universal or expansive common problems in favor of "small-is-beautiful" cutesy commons. These measures (described above as "commons dressing") are carried out both by local people caring for their environment, but also mirrored and recuperated by local authorities, public and private landlords. This is arguably because anything larger, actual large-scale investment in the common good, would potentially threaten house prices and the privatization of wealth that high property values ensure.

With the retreat of the state from any vestige of progressive universalism, self-organized arguments and actions increasingly limit themselves only to self-interested identarian or localist claims. This is contributing to a logic of enclaves, archipelagos, or enclosures expanding globally.[39] Seen alongside each other, the suspicion cannot help but emerge that the ameliorative "commons" developing alongside rapacious forms of private development are not contradictory but complementary. Small-scale commons provide only limited suspensions of private property (e.g., free books, access to vacant sites, communal parks, and gardens). Whether we would like to see this as a generalization or distortion of ecological activism, we must face the grim reality that this is a form of activism, and as Neil Smith has it, "[i]f gentrification is emancipatory political practice, it is difficult to see it as anything other than political activism *against* the working class."[40] Beside them roll out massive processes of asset stripping and looting of social resources, exploiting far more expansive and devastating forms of exception to legal norms, without which profit would be limited and perhaps even unobtainable. Indeed, under the national crisis of the COVID-19 pandemic, small-is-beautiful and "cute" have become instrumental to disaster capitalism.[41] "Aestheticizing powerlessness" not only effectively steers our attention away from monitoring the complex systems we need to sustain our lives, it also maintains, distributes, and extends powerlessness.[42]

---

39. For cogent arguments around this tendency, see Stavros Stavrides, *Common Space: The City as Commons* (London: Zed Books, 2016), 13–29.

40. Smith, *The New Urban Frontier*, 41.

41. Lewis Gordon, "Disaster Aesthetics: How COVID-19 Made the World 'Cute,'" *Art Review*, August 12, 2020, https://artreview.com/disaster-aesthetics-how-covid-19-made-the-world-cute/.

42. Sianne Ngai, quoted in Gordon, "Disaster Aesthetics."

"Commons-longing" can be understood here as one of many political consequences of the retreat of the social democratic state, but also, a recuperation of the shared recent memories of lives less mediated by private property. Yet, this ameliorative nostalgia for something *vaguely like* the commons jettisons the possibility of more aggressive forms of struggle. Lost in this trajectory is the possibility of a commons-based critique of the disciplinary aspects of the welfare state, as well, crucially, as the always-emerging classed, raced, and gendered particularities which produces its most forthright sufferers and critics. With the state-directed disaster of Grenfell Tower (and numerous smaller fires in multiple occupancy dwellings before and since), one can perceive clearly the complex and embattled object which social housing in the UK has become.[43] It is both a resource absolutely necessary to reproducing those most vulnerable in society through which some autonomy and dignity can be attained, and a site of responsibility absolutely incompatible with the present composition of capital.

From Commons to Unenclosure

[C]ontinually capital itself finds things falling out of its orbit, as human beings find use for what exchange value found waste, but rarely does use hold out against the transition to value.
—Peter Porcupine, "Footnote: Defending the Commons"

[A]rt is redeemed time, that is, labour freed of compulsion and open to a sensuous, undetermined relationship to the world. Art therefore is viewed as holding a space for the future in its very negation of the present. It is the potential 'practical criticism' inherent in art's experimental attitude to materials and social relations not organised around coerced labour, instrumental reason and the capitalist accumulation which they make possible.
—Marina Vishmidt, "All Shall Be Unicorns: About Commons, Aesthetics and Time"

In a self-consciously marginal intervention in the revival of the theme of commons in the UK in the 1990s, Peter Porcupine, writing for the Situationist-inspired journal *Here and Now*, argues for commons as a third term, as neither

---

43. Architects for Social Housing, "The Truth about Grenfell Tower: A Report by Architects for Social Housing" (July 21, 2017), https://architectsforsocialhousing.co.uk/2017/07/21/the-truth-about-grenfell-tower-a-report-by-architects-for-social-housing/.

use nor exchange value. This negative positioning of commons vis-à-vis capital's categories resonates closely with art, in Marina Vishmidt's formulation, as an "experimental attitude to materials and social relations not organised around coerced labour, instrumental reason and the capitalist accumulation which they make possible."[44] Commons would then be entities not divisible into resources, not separable from experience. "Only when purified of appropriation would things be colourful and useful at once."[45] Rather than affirm *use* against *exchange*, Peter Porcupine's prickly piece argues that "the left remains gripped by alternative resource management." Instead of criticizing encroachment on human experience, the left aspires to manage, and this logic amounts to simply "arguing for public rather than private enclosure."[46] From this perspective, there is then a world of difference between the strategy of *unenclosure* and the establishment of socialism. Is there a path to full social reproduction which refuses a choice between small-is-beautiful gestures of impotence and "jet-set willy" left accelerationism?

Political geographer Erik Swyngedouw has pioneered an approach to environmental problems which recognizes the ways "the specter of ecological annihilation" is "quilted systematically by the continuous invocation of fear and danger."[47] This means we are unable to grasp what is already happening—"the apocalypse of the present"—in anything other than depoliticized ways which preclude actual change of the organization of society or environment.

> Water conflicts, struggles for food, environmental refugees, etc. testify to the socio-ecological predicament that choreographs everyday life for the majority of the world's population. Things are already too late; they have always already been too late. There is no Arcadian place, time, or environment to return to, no benign socio-ecological past that needs to be maintained or stabilized. Many already live in the interstices of the apocalypse, albeit a combined and uneven one. It is only within the realization of the apocalyptic reality of the now that a new politics might emerge.[48]

---

44. Marina Vishmidt, "All Shall Be Unicorns."
45. Theodor W. Adorno, "Toy Shop," in *Minima Moralia: Reflections on a Damaged Life*, trans. E. F. N. Jephcott (London and New York: Verso, 1974), 228.
46. Peter Porcupine, "Footnote: Defending the Commons," *Here and Now* 14 (1993): 61.
47. Erik Swyngedouw, "Apocalypse Now! Fear and Doomsday Pleasures," *Capitalism Nature Socialism* 24, no.1 (2013): 9–18, 15.
48. Swyngedouw," Apocalypse Now!," 15.

As environmentalists and conservationists have found, rather than "a common treasury for all" the earth is, for capital, but one vast finite resource to be mined to exhaustion. Or, as Anna Tsing has reflected, "Like a giant bulldozer, capitalism appears to flatten the earth to its specifications."[49] Yet, Tsing observes, underneath, or rather, *besides* this apparent flattening, the earth's composition under the supposedly total domination of late-capitalist supply chains is "surprisingly full of cultural variety."[50]

One crucial but often invisible aspect complicating the phantasmagoria of capital's 'total domination' inheres in the linguistic work, which takes place in struggles over the commons. This rings true time and again in urban struggles around community spaces and housing, as we find communities firstly addled by years of underinvestment and disrepair which are then followed by derogatory press and image-based campaigns in the run-up to and during displacement. On the opposing side, which is often far better resourced in terms of communications infrastructure (press, billboards, TV, promotional videos, marketing brochures, etc.), linguistic tricks are a key dimension in overcoming the contradictions of a process designed to make the poor poorer.[51] These tricks need to be revealed and undone through not only pragmatic letter-writing campaigns, petitions, and self-organization (the very fuel of aggressive legal contestation), but also imaginative writing which can communicate the felt experience and joy of being there and staying put. A recent example of aggressive strategies of unenclosure would be the 2021 Berlin referendum, *Deutsche Wohnen & Co. enteignen* [Expropriate Deutsche Wohnen & Co.], seeking to expropriate and socialize over 240,000 apartments in the city of Berlin. While unlikely to be successful in turning over a tightly controlled neoliberal rule of law, the social success and threat of this campaign to the status quo remains palpable. In terms of art, successful projects often spring from embedded campaigns and political cultures, they are a part of that culture, because politics worthy of that name, which is not guided by the self-interest and dishonesty of the status quo's politricks, is a culture sharing dynamism, flexibility, and

49. Anna Tsing, *The Mushroom at the End of the World* (Princeton, NJ: Princeton University Press, 2015), 61.

50. Tsing, *The Mushroom at the End of the World*, 62.

51. For example, as Richard Whitby deftly points out, "Regeneration means the entrance into the Christian state of salvation as a new beginning of life, involving also the abandonment of the former mode of existence as well as the far-reaching consequences of the course entered upon." See Whitby, "Angels, the Phoenix, Bats, Battery Hens and Vultures."

layering of meaning in struggles, providing resources upon which to draw, connecting a past, present, and future and making them vibrate with living tension and impersonal expression.

By way of conclusion, and in counterpoint to some of the more nefarious examples offered above, I shortly gloss some examples from the other side of the barricades, *ours*, where art appeared in the midst of scenes of at least somewhat 'successful' resistance to urban development: Lorraine O'Grady's *Art Is . . .* (1983); Tamara Stoll's *Ridley Road Market* (2019); Crossbones Graveyard (2007–); Anon., *Los Property Developers No Pasarán* (2019); and Lorraine Leeson and Peter Dunn (with others), *Docklands Community Poster Project* (1981–1991).[52] Where art and culture approach a state which can be compared to the commons as a field of social feeling, in which social contradictions, ambiguities, and not-value circulate and are allowed to simply *be* valid and validating of their circuits. These projects touch or explode what I call—after Émile Durkheim's *fait social* or "social facts"—*social questions*, a concentrated site of social meaning, something enigmatic made or produced by the social body which stands to the side of social commentary, instead allowing the social to speak. Where the social stands for itself, not as a transparency but as evidence which is neither self-evident nor easily resolved into identity confirmation. This is to say that art approaches the common when it allows for or foments impersonal expression, when it allows contradictory feelings and situations to visibly unfold. Nevertheless, this must be understood to diverge from affirmation. Art is antisocial at its core; it advances through negations and the refusal of present social consensus.

Lorraine O'Grady's *Art Is . . .* therefore refuses the exclusionary spectacle of policed art: it corrects and negates the common sense consensus that "avant-garde art doesn't have anything to do with Black people," to instead frame, *without making captive*, the anti-spectacle of Black life and joy.[53] Tamara Stoll's photography of Ridley Road Market has to refuse the prevalent mode of the circulation of images in order to invent other

---

52. The *Docklands Community Poster Project* involved a team of collaborators, including graphic designers Sandra Buchanan and Dini Lallah, administrator Belinda Kidd, and contributions by Tony Minion, Sonia Boyce, Donald Rodney, and Keith Piper. See https://cspace.org.uk/category/archive/docklands-community-poster-project.

53. Lorraine O'Grady's *Art Is*, https://lorraineogrady.com/art/art-is.

possible ways of creating images circulating them.[54] The work's location would appear, at first, only coincidental to a subsequent campaign to save the market, "the embodiment of Hackney's diversity and essential to the London Afro-Caribbean community.[55] But to mistake this for coincidence would be precisely to misunderstand and stand apart from the understanding of the market as a place of attractions, deeper connections, and histories.[56] Deep engagement with such spaces shows us exactly how impure and layered a commons can be. On the one hand, the market is simply a municipal commercial resource, managed by the local authority—they want their rents! On the other, it is layered by almost a century of historical meanings and associations, a rich terrain of uncharted gift economies. Here the noncommercial cannot be separated from the commercial, nor can it be the other way around.

The struggle over Crossbones Graveyard is perhaps the clearest example in London of how one might (from my own admittedly isolated regional perspective) envisage a commons and successful strategies for its enduring defense. The site of Crossbones was literally nothing but forgotten history until 2007 when Crossrail, a large-scale state-led railway project acquired the land. From 2007, a seemingly unstemmable tide of incursions, celebrations, and rituals made by a group of local bohemians, witches, and sex workers led to an archeological survey proving that the site was indeed a former unconsecrated burial ground for local sex workers, and following this, to the protection of Crossbones Graveyard in 2017.[57] The campaign involved poetry, direct action, sit-in occupations, magic, gardening, and meet and greets between religious authorities of Southwark Cathedral (who licensed both the original site and, while living and working, those buried there) and local sex workers. *Los Property Developers No Pasarán,* a piece of anonymous graffiti which appeared overnight across the top of the just closed-to-be-demolished Elephant & Castle Shopping Centre, invokes two

---

54. Tamara Stoll, *Ridley Road Market* (self-pub., London, 2019), https://www.tamarastoll.com/Ridley-Road-Market.

55. #SaveRidleyRoad campaign, https://www.saveridleyroad.com/news.

56. For example, the book documents numerous prior attempts to control or expel the market, as well as a rich history of antifascist activity, including the pelting of notable British fascist Oswald Mosely with rotting vegetables. I've written elsewhere on the history of regeneration and gentrification in Hackney, a history which made a struggle over Ridley Road Market more or less inevitable. See Anthony Iles and Benedict Seymour, "The Re-Occupation," *Mute,* January 5, 2006, https://www.metamute.org/editorial/articles/re-occupation.

57. For documentation see Crossbones, https://crossbones.org.uk/.

defeats—that of antifascists in the Spanish Civil War and the loss of the Elephant—but it negates defeat in its cheeky assault on, what was supposed to be for its developers, a secured "asset." Instead, the "Killing of the Elephant" remains a contested process driven by "strong language," and a tenacious campaign led, in particular, by Spanish-speaking communities of South and Central American descent who live, work, and shop around the Elephant.[58] These works each then ride on, flow into, and enrich an existing stream of resistance.

The *Docklands Community Poster Project* flowed into the stream of resistance which had long emanated from the tight-knit dockworkers community of the Isle of Dogs. The *Poster Project's* agit-prop interventions resounded with a sequence of mythic actions which came before and then accompanied their billboards; such as the performative secession via a Universal Declaration of Independence of the Island community in 1970,[59] a protest flotilla, the People's Armada to Parliament in 1985,[60] and the invasion by bees and sheep of a champagne reception held to celebrate the signing of the master build agreement for Canary Wharf attended by the Governor of the Bank of England.[61] The Docklands was for certain a class defeat and one of the battles which cemented the neoliberal restructuring of London, but the locals' campaign secured concessions (affordable housing, open leisure spaces, and community and children's facilities) which now look enviable in comparison with subsequent rounds of regeneration elsewhere in the city.

---

58. For example, see: Southwark Notes (@Southwark Notes), "Anti-Gentrification Histories of The Elephant & Castle in Three Graffiti Acts," January 7, 2019, https://twitter.com/SouthwarkNotes/status/1082282103058898944. For another key piece of imaginative writing involved in this struggle, see Anonymous, "The Killing of the Elephant and Destruction of the Castle," *Anguish Language* (2015), https://anguishlanguage.tumblr.com/tagged/Elephant-%26-Castle.

59. Ian Bone, "March 1st, 1970 – ISLE OF DOGS DECLARES INDEPENDENCE!," *Ian Bone*, August 5, 2009, https://ianbone.wordpress.com/2009/08/05/march-1st-1970-isle-of-dogs-declares-independence/amp/.

60. Mike Brooke, "Even Thames Armada and sheep couldn't stop Docklands invasion of Isle of Dogs," *East London Advertiser*, October, 2, 2017, https://www.eastlondonadvertiser.co.uk/news/even-thames-armada-and-sheep-couldn-t-stop-docklands-invasion-3571848.

61. For the *Poster Project's* photodocumentation of this campaign, see cSPACE, https://cspace.org.uk/archive/campaigns/.

FIGURE 2.4. *Mike Seaborne, The Docklands Armada Boat at the Houses of Parliament,* Docklands Community Poster Project, *1986. © Photo by Mike Seaborne, 1986.*

It is with humor, collective joy, reversals of power, and a thorough trampling of the enemy's resources that such concessions are extracted. Alongside and with the fixation upon particular spaces and cultures, we need to develop practices, techniques, and strategies of *unenclosure* as activity which overthrows through *negation*, rather than founding through *affirmation*. There is always therefore a third thing, which has no use, no instrumental reason attached to it which is key to the commons and key to the struggles to both defend and expand them.

Lauren Berlant approached the recent use of the concept of commons critically, noting that while politics is becoming "identical" with the "reinvention of infrastructures for managing the unevenness, ambivalence, violence, and ordinary contingency of contemporary existence," the commons may, as a concept, seek to smooth over in advance problematic aspects of our common experience, objects which our politics should bear upon not deflect from.[62] Berlant warns against using the commons concept as a way

---

62. Lauren Berlant, "The Commons: Infrastructures for troubling times," *Environment and Planning D: Society and Space* 34, no. 3 (2016): 393–419.

of providing holistic but false solutions by "positivizing the ambivalence that saturates social life about the irregular conditions of fairness."[63] Rather, this ambivalence and our endlessly mutating relation to class (to domination and power, forms of separation, inclusion and exclusion, community and social isolation) needs to be held central to our experience and to our needs for commons. False or compensatory commons seek to artificially overcome these separations and uncomfortable mediations. Instead, we should celebrate, defend, preserve, and extend commons as spaces of difference, and also, as spaces that can support and sustain difference and unmanageability. Commons may be approached by language, but like language they inhere without us, as manifestly social but also indifferent. We may use them, we can contribute to them, we couldn't exist without them, but their beauty and consistency is in their ongoing existence despite and without us.

Addendum: A Glossary of Concepts on Commons

What follows is a series of glosses, or commentaries, on concepts which provide theoretical support for this chapter and offers the reader a means with which to critically explore the contested territory over which commons spill. At times polemical and at others measured, it asserts that human arrangements for living as much as ideas about what might make living "good"are the mutable work of history.

Gentrification

> One by one, many of the working-class quarters of London have been invaded by the middle classes—upper and lower. Once this process of 'gentrification' starts in a district it goes on rapidly until all or most of the original working-class occupiers are displaced and the whole social character of the district is changed.
> —Ruth Glass, *London: Aspects of Change* (1964)

A few observations: Glass' formulation of gentrification is useful because it described an apparently organic or informal phenomenon taking place separately or to the side of top-down, state-led reconstruction of cities in

---

63. Berlant, "The Commons."

the postwar period. It should be noted that this view of gentrification as organic and informal has been sharply contested. Neil Smith has countered this "consumer sovereignty hypothesis" with the forceful and consistent argument that "gentrification is a structural product of the land and housing markets."[64] He also highlights the state's role in early gentrification schemes in the US and emphasizes the state as the facilitator of the conditions which make gentrification a "social product."

In Glass' formulation, gentrification as process has a telos; it is inevitable and suggests a complete rather than incomplete transformation. This *doxa* has been passed down as the lore of gentrification, echoed in the words of landlord-novelist Chris Kraus, "gentrification is inevitable."[65] However, no social phenomenon viewed as a historical process is "inevitable" or irreversible. The precondition for cycles of boom are often cycles of bust and devaluation (as Smith shows). We may not be in control of these processes, but if the value of property can expand exponentially it must then also be possible for it to deflate. As I explore throughout the chapter, deflation and inflation are necessary poles in development cycles.

Urban Regeneration

Peter Roberts describes urban regeneration as "comprehensive and integrated vision and action which leads to the resolution of urban problems, and which seeks to bring about a lasting improvement in the economic, physical, social, and environmental condition of an area that has been subject to change.[66]

---

64. Neil Smith, "Toward a Theory of Gentrification: A Back to the City Movement by Capital, not People," *Journal of the American Planning Association* 45, no. 4 (1979): 538 and 546.

65. Chris Kraus' pronouncement was made at a seminar held in January 2015 at Central Saint Martin's, University of the Arts London. At the seminar and subsequent events, Kraus drew the ire of critics and housing activists with close experience of processes of gentrification in the US and the UK. A subsequent public event at which she appeared in New York was disrupted. See Jillian Billard, "Art & Gentrification: What is 'Artwashing' and What Are Galleries Doing to Resist It?," *Artspace Magazine*, November, 30, 2017; *Artforum* News, "Boyle Heights Gallery Event Canceled After Activists Threatened to Disrupt It," *Artforum*, October, 11, 2017.
   A good introduction to LA artist-activist group Boyle Heights Alliance Against Artwashing and Displacement (BHAAAD) is provided in their pamphlet "The Short History of a Long Struggle" (2016), *Southwark Notes*, https://southwarknotes.files.wordpress.com/2012/03/bhaaad-pamphlet-paginated.pdf.

66. Peter Roberts and Hugh Sykes, eds., *Urban Regeneration: A Handbook* (London, Thousand Oaks, New Delhi: Sage, 2000).

Unstated, but generally understood, is the fact that regeneration is a state-led or state-directed process. It may—or in fact always does—benefit real estate speculators, private developers, construction firms, and other contractors, but in general to achieve their ends requires the state's mediation.[67] With urban regeneration, the state becomes a key actor in establishing the private and public agencies and conditions through which cultural gentrification will take place. These measures include parcelling, compulsorily purchasing and then reselling land to large developers, land remediation, rezoning, targeted cultural funding, the local state leasing commercial spaces at subsidized rents to cultural agents, and specific tax discounts for particular property types favored for cultural uses. Drilling down further, we could understand urban regeneration as a form of privatization or asset-stripping which necessarily requires the state as a central but vanishing mediator. The state has to act in order to divest itself and become smaller.

In Roberts' statement, the key elements which distinguish the intentional and generally state-led phenomenon of regeneration from gentrification is the "comprehensive and integrated" character of these processes. However, taking in Smith's argument, we might simply argue that regeneration is the state becoming self-conscious, more directly engaged, and explicit in its tendency to facilitate profitable urban development. "Improvement" is subjective rather than objective; that is, this depends on who is doing the improving and for whom it benefits. Secondly, the lasting nature of regeneration projects can and has been increasingly put in question by social movements and academic critics. However, watch out, in the UK context, "failed regeneration" frequently begets future regeneration schemes. Regeneration is a supposedly more stable and coherent project than gentrification, and thus more easily made an object of critique.

Enclosure

Enclosure describes the process of fencing and globalization of land taking place in the British Isles from the twelfth century and intensifying

---

67. This is, however, somewhat different from Smith's definition of gentrification. In Smith's model, the state parcels land, makes a favorable legal environment, and arranges the general conditions for developers and the real estate market to flourish. Regeneration presupposes gentrification will arrive but involves a synthesis of the cultural and economic theories of gentrification.

in the sixteenth to the eighteenth centuries. Enclosures sought to replace and revoke a system of customary rights over commons enjoyed by commoners, whereby social reproduction was ensured through the free and seasonal access to land for grazing, water, fish, wood, and other necessities. "Enclosure is the historical antonym and nemesis of the commons," writes Peter Linebaugh, arguing that accompanying the piecemeal process of enclosure was an exponential growth in crimes pertaining to property and carceral institutions developed to imprison transgressors of the new property regime.[68] The act of enclosing commons made commoners dependent on wage work for sustenance, thus was the commoner made vagrant or proletarian. Deviation from wage work—attempt to survive by what had now become "theft"—made them subject to imprisonment.

Commons

Commons describe, in a literal sense, the actual land enclosed in the above definition. These were not, in fact, absolutely outside of any form of ownership, but even if owned by a local lord or parish, the rights to access and to customary use of the land as a resource pulled it outside the singular and exclusive access by which we understand property. Marx was explicit in his conjoining of the theft of common land and the creation of a "supply" of landless proletariat to industrial capitalism. These are understood to be twinned and combined developments:

> The spoliation of the church's property, the fraudulent alienation of the State domains, the robbery of the common lands, the usurpation of feudal and clan property, and its transformation into modern private property under circumstances of reckless terrorism, were just so many idyllic methods of primitive accumulation. They conquered the field for capitalistic agriculture, made the soil part and parcel of capital, and created for the town industries the necessary supply of a 'free' and outlawed proletariat.[69]

68. Peter Linebaugh, *Stop, Thief! The Commons, Enclosures, and Resistance* (Oakland: PM Press, 2014), 1.

69. Karl Marx, *Capital, Vol. 1: A Critique of Political Economy*, trans. Samuel Moore and Edward Aveling (New York: Modern Library, 1906).

Commons were not simply the soil, but also the air, water, wood, and fish which they supported. Ensuring access to these prerequisites in turn supported the commoners and tied them to the land and place, the source of their social reproduction. The commons as a metaphor has since extended to encompass everything from squats to women's bodies, to file-sharing sites, unpatented seeds, and plants every air we breathe. The vagueness of commons-as-a-metaphor, however, can begin to appear problematic. Commoning is a practice of fulfilling social reproduction directly, or *unenclosing*, and making common certain spaces or resources. It must be grasped as a verb and not only as a metaphor.

New Enclosures

"New enclosures" is a concept coined by US-autonomist Marxist group and journal Midnight Notes in 1990 to encompass the global wave of proletarianization coinciding with the end of "really existing socialism" after 1989. This was an agile attempt to proletarianize class, environment, race, gender, labor, and nature at a moment when postmodernists were still proclaiming the death of such "master categories." Rather then, all this was becoming reconfigured. Capitalism, without a clear opposing ideology, was poised to ravage the globe beyond previous limits extending and intensifying the range of its exploitative forms of accumulation. In a text introducing their concept of new enclosures, Midnight Notes writes:

> According to the Marxist tradition, the Enclosures were the starting point of capitalist society. They were the basic device of 'original accumulation' which created a population of workers 'free' from any means of reproduction and thus compelled (in time) to work for a wage. The Enclosures, however, are not a one-time process exhausted at the dawn of capitalism. They are a regular return on the path of accumulation and a structural component of class struggle.[70]

The uptake of Midnight Notes' formulation of the new enclosures and the revival of commons discourses fed into the recomposition of global social movements around issues of land, labor, feminism, housing, intellectual

---

70. Midnight Notes, "Introduction to the New Enclosures," *Midnight Notes* 10 (Jamaica Plain, MA: Midnight Notes, 1990): 1.

property regimes, and the environment, under the cycle of struggles known as the anti- or alter-globalization movement. This was both an attempt to renew Marxian theory to address this new phase of capitalist accumulation and develop a theory of globalization updating the notions of development pioneered in socialist countries under the rubric of *diamat* (dialectical materialism).

Primitive, Originary, or Primary Accumulation

Within the concept of "new enclosures" was a specific reading of Marx's category of "primitive accumulation," also known as "originary" or "primary" accumulation. Formulated in *Capital, Vol. 1*, Marx uses the concept to dispel the idea that capitalists earned their capital by hard work, rather indicating that the initial accumulation which facilitated the institution of property is indeed the source of poverty. Enclosure is the event that propels free men into unfree wage labor, and "the history of this, their expropriation, is written in the annals of mankind in letters of blood and fire."[71] Midnight Notes' innovation followed an emergent and unorthodox reading developed by translator, editor, printer, and publisher Fredy Perlman, who argued, against the orthodox Marxist model of development then dominant:

> The primitive or preliminary accumulation of capital is not something that happened once, in the distant past, and never after. It is something that continues to accompany the capitalist production process, and is an integral part of it. Without an ongoing primitive accumulation of capital, the production process would stop; each crisis would tend to become permanent.[72]

Informing Perlman's openly transhistorical (but not ahistorical) concept of primitive accumulation was his own research into debates between Marxist economists directing post-revolutionary development in the Soviet Union. Perlman discovered not only that the models of production and

---

71. Marx, *Capital*, 876.
72. Fredy Perlman, "The Continuing Appeal of Nationalism," *Fifth Estate* (Winter 1984), https://theanarchistlibrary.org/library/fredy-perlman-the-continuing-appeal-of-nationalism.

management in the Soviet Union were primarily capitalist and American, i.e., Taylorist, but also that Soviet Marxists, led by Yevgeni Preobrazhensky, had experimented with ideas of "socialist primitive accumulation," which they conceived as an expropriative and exploitative process necessary to build a powerful socialist state. While Preobrazhenky and colleagues may have seen this as a socialist alternative, for Marxists such as Perlman and Amadeo Bordiga (who formulated similar views as early as the 1950s), such information confirmed the capitalist orientation of the Bolshevik state and its achievement of an alternative path to bourgeois revolution and, eventually, capitalist states in Russia and Eastern Europe.

In a post-Cold War context, Midnight Notes argued that the new enclosures were a form of continuous primitive accumulation; and that this was not only a phenomenon taking place at the peripheries of capitalism (in the so-called Third World), Under the same logic of direct appropriation of social resources, Midnight Notes warned, capitalists would launch attacks at home in the West just as they did abroad at the far reaches of the unfolding capitalist empire:

> [F]or every factory in a free-trade zone in China privatized and sold to a New York commercial bank, or for every acre enclosed by a World Bank development project in Africa or Asia as part of a 'debt for equity' swap, a corresponding enclosure must occur in the U.S. and Western Europe.[73]

That these processes are indeed linked remains a fertile area to explore, but how? And whether they are indeed balanced and reciprocal, as Midnight Notes suggests, remains a seductive, speculative, but as yet unproven thesis.

Accumulation by Dispossession

In a related development, David Harvey, whose close reading of *Capital* has become a key resource for many coming to Marx's texts anew in search of an analysis of the complexities of late capitalism, formulated the concept of "accumulation by dispossession." It draws upon Marx's concept of primitive accumulation but attempts to remove its relation to the past and rather understand it as a tendency specific to the phase of neoliberal accumulation. In a rereading of economic history since the 1970s, Harvey came

---

73. Midnight Notes, "Introduction to the New Enclosures," 2.

to understand neoliberalism as a response to a profit and overaccumulation crisis. For Harvey, neoliberal capitalism doesn't so much generate wealth as redistribute it upwards, to the upper classes:

> By this I mean the continuation and proliferation of accumulation practices which Marx had treated of as 'primitive' or 'original' during the rise of capitalism., These include the commodification and privatization of land and the forceful expulsion of peasant populations [. . .]; conversion of various forms of property rights (common, collective, state, etc.) into exclusive property rights [. . .] suppression of rights to the commons; commodification of labour power and the suppression of alternative (indigenous) forms of production and consumption [. . .] and, most devastating of all, the use of the credit system as a radical means of accumulation by dispossession.[74]

A weakness of Harvey's account is that it suggests a normative model of capitalism is possible; that neoliberalism is somehow a deviation from it, rather than its continuation by other means. This is not necessarily Harvey's reading, rather, it is a problem of emphasis. Harvey develops his account of capitalist political economy of the last forty years from the combination of empirical study and the renewals of Marx's categories and systematic account. In combination with concepts such as the "spatial fix" (investment in space as a solution to internal crises), Harvey reads capitalist urbanism as providing a key sector of profit and reorganization of capital as a solution to late capitalism's inability to presently derive sufficient profits from productive industry.

Spatial Deconcentration

"Spatial deconcentration" is a concept developed by Midnight Notes following the work of murdered housing activist Yulanda Ward in Washington, DC. It is named after a US government program which sought to expel urban Black populations concentrated in cities across the US. In the shift from a phase of Fordism (industrial capitalism based on large-scale manufacture) to post-Fordism (development of service work, technology, communications, and finance) the "spatial concentration" of proletarian

---

74. David Harvey, *A Brief History of Neoliberalism* (Oxford: Oxford University Press, 2011), 159.

populations in cities, segregated and divided along raced and classed lines in order to serve a particular industrial division of labor, switches into forms of spatial deconcentration. Urban areas and their populations are first abandoned and devalued, then attacked and displaced by new rounds of inward investment and speculation. This corresponds to David Harvey's presentation of the mutability of space and fixed forms under capitalism:

> Capital necessarily creates a physical landscape in its own image at one point in time only to have to destroy it at some later point in time as it pursues geographical expansions and temporal displacements as solutions to the crises of overaccumulation to which it is regularly prone.[75]

Of consequence as we begin to understand the shifting and lurching interests of capitalism is the way this affects the valuation of urban terrain. As crises loom, capitalists seek to preserve their capital by finding areas for safe investment. With deindustrialization money flowed out of US and UK cities. Housing in these contexts often became less and less valuable as populations also left for lack of jobs. However, at a later point, with a return to investment in inner cities (often as a result of capital fleeing profits crises in other sectors and areas), an opportune "rent gap" might appear, for example, between a low-income neighborhood and a high-income neighborhood.

Rent Gap

The "rent gap" is a key term in a set of debates around gentrification in US cities. Developed by Neil Smith, it forms a cornerstone in his theory of uneven development and was a crucial tool in displacing cultural and consumption-based explanations for cycles of gentrification, displacement, and speculative investment in favor of more capital-based or production-based explanatory theories.[76] There is a technical aspect to Smith's strict definition of the rent gap (pertaining to how ground rent operates in US cities), however, I think a slightly looser definition still helps us understand cycles of gentrification and redevelopment generally.

---

75. David Harvey, "The 'New Imperialism': Accumulation by Dispossession," *Socialist Register* 40 (2004): 66.

76. See Neil Smith, *The New Urban Frontier: Gentrification and the Revanchist City* (New York: Routledge, 2005), 38–41.

The rent gap is the disparity between the potential ground rent level and the actual ground rent capitalized under the present land use (Figure 3.2). The rent gap is produced primarily by capital devalorization (which diminishes the proportion of the ground rent able to be capitalized) and also by continued urban development and expansion (which has historically raised the potential ground rent level in the inner city).[77] For Smith, gentrification is always preceded by a period of devalorization, and this means there is a potential difference in price between real estate assets in one area and in another. There are a number of potential developments (transport, cultural events, university expansions, museums, galleries, new parks) which developers and real estate speculators might know about ahead of the general public. Therefore, these opportunities for exploiting the difference between prices in one area or another are frequently the cause of gentrification. Investors and developers have developed tools and techniques to exploit these differences to the maximum: land banking, lobbying for the changing of zoning laws, dramatically raising rents, bringing in artists, etc. Essentially by acquiring and then sitting on valuable land or real estate in an organized way, investors can manipulate differences in value by buying cheap, manipulating the appeal of an area, then selling high. Within these cycles there is also a vested interest in landlords not spending their income on repairs, moving from responding to the apparently "natural" occurrence of rent gaps, interested operators begin to "produce for themselves the conditions and opportunity for a whole new round of capital reinvestment."[78] We see this phenomena on a local scale worldwide, but it is crucial to understand it within the circuit of these larger dynamics tracked by the concepts above.

Capitalist Commoning

Just as there is a model of "socialist primitive accumulation" so there can be a model of "capitalist commoning." In Peter Linebaugh's initial formulation, "[t]he South Sea Bubble was the wreck of a kind of capitalist commoning."[79] Through his account we are led to understand that the murky legal measures which led to the rapid inflation of one of the first global financial

---

77. Smith, *New Urban Frontier*, 65.
78. Smith, *New Urban Frontier*, 21.
79. Linebaugh, "Charters of Liberty in Black Face and White Face."

bubbles in the 1720s (backed by the expectation of unlimited new profits from slavery) brought together the necessary legal and fiscal powers within a framework which would facilitate the empowerment of the state in order to furnish "needs of capital as a whole" over those of individual capitals.[80] This assembly of fiscal and legal powers in the hands of the national state, over and against the power of individual capitals, and local, state, or workers' representatives, is something we see in regeneration projects, megaprojects (such as the Olympics), colonial or neocolonial endeavors, and wars.

I have used the concept of "capitalist commoning" to describe the way the state acquires the legal right to parcel up land around a large-scale process of urban development, or even acquires then remediates land at the cost of the taxpayer, before passing it onto private developers to profit from the rent gap (the difference in value between before and after this process). Similarly, developers form enormous consortiums to leverage capital (borrow money cheaply) from sources such as pension funds and therefore acquire land on a scale, and for prices, which no other competitor (even the state) can obtain. The London Docklands, the city's second financial center, received an estimated £900 million in public funding to build an entirely private business zone surrounded by water and protected by private security and bylaws controlling normal access rights. This is the first meaning of "capitalist commoning." A second meaning could perhaps be applied to the increasing integration of affirmative and conspicuous small-is-beautiful practices, such as urban gardening, cooking, pickling, knitting, and so on. As with the first, we will see that what is decisive is whether practices of commoning actively disrupt and antagonize capitalist categories of property, money, and wage labor, or whether they seek accommodation within or complementarity to them.

Financialization, or Capital's Spatial Fix

Capital's need for transportation, communication, and storage structure space and the environment.[81] It is through these "spatial fixes" that capitalism produces value and then later disaggregates it in order to provide for new areas of innovation, opportunity, and profit.[82] In postwar Europe,

---

80. Linebaugh, "Charters of Liberty in Black Face and White Face."
81. Henri Lefebvre, *The Production of Space* (Oxford and Cambridge: Blackwell, 1991).
82. David Harvey, "The Spatial Fix: Hegel, von Thunen and Marx," *Antipode* 13, no. 3 (1981): 1–12.

on either side of the "Iron Curtain," such spatial fixes were introduced as large-scale urban restructuring processes, organized by states that felt the pressures of reconstructing cities ravaged by war. Employed within these relatively unified programs of public works, art was integrated, for the first time, as exceptional and autonomous, seemingly serving the purpose of no purpose, e.g., spiritually edifying public art, albeit within a context tailored to the needs of industrial capitalist development.[83] Later, "spatial fixes" become the response to crises of overaccumulation[84] and temporary solutions to the destructive effects of competition—driving the "annihilation of space by time"—achieved by earlier revolutions in transport and communications.[85] At this point spatial commodification develops from being a corollary of industrial development—with some speculative activity in railways and real estate in the nineteenth century—into a core area of accumulation in the late twentieth and early twenty-first centuries due to the increasing prominence of global finance.[86]

It is through these macro-dynamics unfolding globally, according to Michael Hudson and Loren Goldner, that finance ceases to serve investment in productive industry and becomes the central motor of (and in fact barrier to) development as financialization. It determines the form through which first corporations, then almost all enterprises of every form and function, both large and small, reproduce themselves.[87] Within this emergent field of intense global competition between cities, vying to solicit investment from the swarm of "nomad dollars,"[88] seeking profit worldwide,

83. See, for example, the debates around the exclusion of industrial art in the postwar formation of the Arts Council of England in Michael T. Saler, *The Avant-Garde in Interwar England: Medieval Modernism and the London Underground* (Oxford: Oxford University Press, 2001), 167–169. Notable here is John Maynard Keynes' dual role in the integration of art and, importantly, artists into the state as an exception to the general division of labor in society and his central importance to the economic reform of the postwar state generally. See also Roberts, "Table of the Evolution of Urban Regeneration," 14.

84. Henri Lefebvre, *The Survival of Capitalism* (London: Allison & Busby/St Martin's Press, 1976).

85. Karl Marx, *Grundrisse: Foundations of the Critique of Political Economy* (New York: Vintage, 1973), 538.

86. Costas Lapavitsas, "Financialisation, or the Search for Profits in the Sphere of Circulation," *SOAS*, May 11, 2009, http://www.soas.ac.uk/rmf/papers/file51263.pdf.

87. See Loren Goldner, "Fictitious Capital for Beginners: Imperialism, 'Anti-Imperialism, and the Continuing Relevance of Rosa Luxemburg," *Mute* 2, no. 6 (August 21, 2007); Michael Hudson, *Super Imperialism: The Origin and Fundamentals of U.S. World Dominance* (London: Pluto Press, 2003).

88. Goldner, "Fictitious Capital for Beginners."

urbanization becomes a key mediator and art is at stake within it.[89] David Harvey and many others following him have argued that within these new finance-driven forms of rentier urbanism, culture and art, design and architecture become commodifiable markers of authenticity and uniqueness.[90] In the nineteenth century, art and artists had gained their autonomy in the initial period of industrial expansion coupled with redevelopment of the inner city, where art is a crucial and critical means of envisioning and reflecting on those rapid changes as they happen. Subsequently, in the state-directed appropriation of the tools of civic redevelopment in the 1950s, artistic modernism was brought inside the process and inside the state. In the 1960s and '70s, with the growth of a finance, insurance, and real estate-led economy (FIRE), artists explore these new organizational processes as media and as modes of organization.[91] This provides us with the credible linkages between finance and urbanization which structure our framework, as well as the periodization of art within capital's self-development.

In turn, the question of whether art is outside or inside these economic processes themselves becomes moot or at least murky. Artists strive for and continue to invent forms of autonomy and criticality, but at the same time they are increasingly exposed to and integrated into the densely capitalized environment in which they practice and live. From the 1970s to the present, artists are increasingly conceived of as economic actors directing these processes or at least assisting them.[92]

---

89. Louis Moreno, "The Urban Process under Financialized Capitalism," *City* 18, no. 3 (2014): 244–268.

90. David Harvey, "The Art of Rent: Globalization, Monopoly and the Commodification of Culture," *Socialist Register* 38 (2002): 98.

91. A key framing of conceptual art in terms of media and information was the exhibition *Information*, curated by Kynaston McShine at Museum of Modern Art, New York City, July 2–September 20, 1970.

92. For a landmark study of the New York art scene and real estate economy's imbrication, see Sharon Zukin, *Loft Living: Culture and Capital in Urban Change* (Baltimore and London: The Johns Hopkins University Press, 1982). For interesting insights into the relationship between deindustrialization, minimalism's fetishization of the industrial, and the emergence of a fabrication economy, see Julia Bryan-Wilson, *Art Workers: Radical Practice in the Vietnam War Era* (Berkeley: University of California Press, 2009). For a more recent study focusing on Europe, see Matteo Pasquinelli, *Animal Spirits: A Bestiary of the Commons* (Rotterdam and Amsterdam: NAi and Institute of Network Cultures, 2008). For an account stressing the involvement and agency of artists, but in *opposition* to institutional forms of redevelopment in the context of Berlin, see Nicola Guy, "Art in the Interim: How the Issue of the Restitution of Housing in Reunified Berlin Led to an Artistic Reimagining of the City," in *Radical Housing: Art, Struggle, Care*, ed. Ana Vilenica (Amsterdam: Institute of Network Cultures, 2021), 152–164. For a survey of artists against regeneration, see activist group Southwark Notes' list, "Artists Working against Gentrification," https://southwarknotes.wordpress.com/art-and-regeneration/artists-against-regen/.

While the process of financialization in symbiosis with urbanization presently maintains some of the characteristics of the rentier city of the nineteenth century, Louis Moreno argues, following Costas Lapavitsas, *this time is different*. We are experiencing not a "cyclical condition" but a qualitative change in capital's "molecular composition," an "unprecedented transformation in the way capital reproduces itself as a global system."[93] These changes, he argues, arise "out of the general entanglement of production and consumption in the sphere of finance. Hence, the causes of transformation of capitalism are to be found at the 'molecular' level of the 'relations of accumulation, rather than in policy or institutional change.'"[94] Indeed, finance begins to implicate austerity everywhere because it accelerates and dynamizes the drive towards ever more "efficient" socially necessary labor time as a component of the process of the production of commodities at a global level. This process destroys the grounds for accumulation in previously stable areas, just as it necessitates outwards expansion to model sectors formerly at a remove from the production of commodities—e.g., art or childcare or the maintenance of social housing—in its own image and on the basis of a restless, and ultimately self-destructive, search for exponential increases in efficiency and profit.

---

93. Moreno, "The Urban Process," 249.
94. Moreno, "The Urban Process," 253.

Chapter 3

A MOVEMENT TO TRANSFORM EVERYTHING: KNOWLEDGE PRODUCTION TOWARDS SOLIDARITY ECONOMY IN HUNGARY

Ágnes Gagyi and Zsuzsanna Pósfai, in conversation with Mary N. Taylor

Three friends came together in 2021 to discuss the knowledge production unfolding in Hungary towards commoning and building a solidarity economy. Tracing ten years of research and action by a network of actors that has led to the development of a first rental cooperative house, the Gólya Cooperative, and the Kazán Community House, Ági and Zsuzsi reflect on the challenges and promises of small research-oriented initiatives, and questions of the commons vs. the solidarity economy. Asking how the observable capacity of people to take care of themselves can be freed from the extractive circuits of capital, they propose tracing relations of value while attempting to build technical solutions, allowing them to enter market relations but work against them and build the social power that can sustain such solutions.

Mary N. Taylor: Zsuzsi, you are an urbanist and one of the cofounders of the Periféria Center, and Ági, you are a sociologist and a cofounder of the Solidarity Economy Center. Together, the two centers are involved in a project to develop something that could be called a "commons" with regard to housing in Budapest. You came to this via your work in groups that are networked together, by drawing on social movement experience, and lots of research and analytical work of different kinds. Can you speak a bit about the practical work, as well as your broader movement experience and research background? What are the goals, accomplishments, challenges, and histories of this initiative?

Zsuzsanna Pósfai [Zsuzsi]: What you are referring to as our project of commoning is mainly work aiming to develop new housing cooperatives; more specifically, rental-based housing cooperatives. The idea of this was born about ten years ago, connected to the broader political context of Fidesz (the rightist party ruling with a two-thirds majority since 2010) coming to power, and our mistrust of the state. In the beginning we imagined physically connected spaces, such as a big building with a community space, a bar, workshop areas, and housing as well. But I don't think any of us called it commoning or commons. It was connected, rather, to the idea of self-determination. The bar and community space (which is Gólya Cooperative today) developed faster and was important for different political movements from 2011 onwards.

After operating for several years in a rented space (from which its name came), Gólya bought a large building on the edge of a huge brownfield site. The public comes together at concerts, performances, workshops, lectures, while several allied organizations also have workspaces. The semi-public, or collectively used space of offices, workshops, daycare, and sports hall (everything but the bar and public space) is now called the Kazán Community House. We are currently working on putting this part of the building into a structure of collective ownership that will guarantee this purpose for its use for the long term.

Meanwhile, the housing idea was constantly there but remained an informal network of people living in shared flats for many years. Around 2012, we started learning more systematically about housing cooperatives, developing organizational, legal, and financial models that could work in our context, partly supported by international contacts and learning from their experiences. In 2016, we started working more seriously on finding a house and in May 2018 we purchased one, moving in January 2019. This house is not a cooperative in the legal sense but functions as one.

FIGURE 3.1. *Gólya Cooperative bar and community space, Budapest. Photo by Gólya Cooperative.*

We also established an Eastern European network of pioneering housing cooperative initiatives, MOBA Housing Network, in January 2018. *Moba* means the same thing in Bosnian/Serbian/Croatian as the Hungarian word *kaláka*. Both refer to collective work and mutual help, whether in agriculture or in building houses. I think we are attached to this name because it really roots the idea of collectivism and mutual aid locally. Moba is a practice that people in Eastern Europe can relate to, and we chose to articulate it in this language because most members of MOBA are from the Balkans. So, it demonstrates our commitment to building on notions and practices that are present in our own societies.

The next step in this process of housing commoning is the establishment of an alternative real estate developer. This is an idea that we came up with sometime in 2020, based on some basic Marxist ideas of the city: that access to property and access to real estate determines, in the end, who has access to space in the city. We felt that we already had some experience in collaborative real estate development, due to Gólya Cooperative having bought and renovated an old industrial building, and due to our experience of having developed the first cooperative house. We call this new organization the Alliance for Collaborative Real Estate Development, and with it, we aim to help different leftist grassroots organizations have access to space and to organize cooperative forms of affordable housing.

Ágnes Gagyi [Ági]: These projects emerged from a shared research trajectory about the current transformations of capitalism and Hungary's place within it, and about the city and real estate in that context. As Zsuzsi mentioned, together with many other organizers of this project we make up a relatively coherent group or network. This network is made of an early cohort of the Hungarian New Left generation who were organizing together, living in these connected flats, taking part in diverse political initiatives together or with others. This same network also gave birth [in 2010] to the Working Group for Public Sociology, *Helyzet* [Position], that has been trying to understand the current social, economic, and political transformations taking place in Hungary already under the first of Fidesz's three consecutive terms (starting in 2010), and how these processes fit into long-term dynamics of global capitalism. Our research in Helyzet has given us tools for understanding our context. This is also true for the research Zsuzsi and others were doing around urban questions.

Mary: Can you speak a bit about this urban research? How is understanding the capitalist production of space useful to understanding urban conditions and how capitalism operates today? How has your research fed into the practical work you do?

Zsuzsi: Our urban research started during our university years in an organization that many of us were members of—the College for Social Theory [*Társadalomelméleti Kollégium*, TEK]—and where some of us initiated a critical urban studies group.[1] One of our first activities was a David Harvey reading group, and we also translated several of his writings to Hungarian. Translating Harvey's "The Right to the City" into Hungarian in 2009

---

1. TEK is not a "college" in the commonly used English-language sense. In Hungary, a college is a group formed around a topic or practice, often in an academic setting. Run by university students, TEK has been and remains important to left knowledge production among university students in Hungary. It can be seen as another node in the network described here, reflected also in its journal *Fordulat* [Turn]; for example, issue 27 was dedicated to questions of the solidarity economy.

was important in my personal learning process.[2] During this time I was also in the activist group *A Város Mindenkié* (AVM) [The City is for All], founded in 2009 by housed and unhoused people influenced by Picture the Homeless in New York City. AVM uses the strategies of advocacy and direct action in the field of housing, and does very important work, both in terms of direct interventions and putting the issue of housing poverty on the political agenda. My frustration with demanding things from a state that would continuously ignore us especially in the hostile environment of the Fidesz government pushed me towards thinking about housing in the framework of the solidarity economy.

Meanwhile, the critical urban studies group continued to work together. In 2012 we edited a critical urban studies reader that introduced important texts to Hungarian speakers and conducted reading circles and workshops and published some articles in the press.[3] After leaving TEK, some of us were pursuing postgraduate degrees or working in research institutions. In 2018, four of us from the group founded the Periféria Center to continue this work in a more professional setting. So, it grew out of this long process of researching urban issues, housing, the production of space, capitalism, and cities together, and also individually, in our different more institutional or activist projects. Periféria Center's research agenda has also developed in conversation with Helyzet, and there are very big personal overlaps between these two groups as well.

Ági: The Solidarity Economy Center (SEC), which is collaborating with Periféria on the housing cooperative project, is another node where we combine research coming out from this network with practical organizing. The SEC has been working since 2019 to build solidarity economy solutions in the fields of energy, food, and housing, and to connect them to union organizing.

Zsuzsi: Our research has fed into the practical work in many ways. Understanding how money goes into fixed space, and into real estate particularly, helps us understand what's happening around us and is also essential for thinking about what you can do differently—about possible points

2. David Harvey, "The Right to the City," *New Left Review* 53 (September/October 2008), https://newleftreview.org/issues/ii53/articles/david-harvey-the-right-to-the-city.
3. Csaba Jelinek, Judit Bodnár, Márton Czirfusz, and Zoltán Ginelli, *Kritikai Városkutatás* (Budapest: L'Harmattan, 2013).

of intervention. I am constantly using what I learned through my PhD research about housing finance, the housing market—even the vocabulary of these companies—in the practical work I do to develop new forms of finance for affordable housing.

When research is used in movement building it becomes a tool to frame things for others as well. I have a very powerful story from when I was still a member of AVM, and we were working to organize the residents of a few housing blocks that were going to be demolished because of a big real estate project. One of the guys that we were speaking to was going to be evicted, and the issue was how much and what kind of compensation they would get from the municipality. He basically explained rent gap theory in his own words: how the developer will have much more profit than what he receives as compensation. In such a situation, theoretical knowledge and research can be a tool for verifying peoples' experiences. My experience at AVM is very much part of my research trajectory, and I do think it would be very beneficial for proponents of the "advocacy strategy" and of the "housing commons strategy" to think more about their complementarities and potential linkages.

Mary: You're describing praxis, the relationship between theory and practice and the ways in which they drive one another. This dialectic over time seems to have a lot to do with your arrival to the question of the solidarity economy as you made your way to solidifying Gólya as a cooperative with its own building and developing the first rental housing cooperative. In fact, your practice continues to be a kind of research.

Ági: Yes, we were interested in how capitalism works within the Hungarian environment where we were trying to do politics from the left, but also quite connected to this magic of doing things autonomously. This is how we became interested in how informal reproductive capacity interacts with capitalist extraction, and how the state regulates what is formal and what is informal, legal or illegal, and sets the value of interactions in terms of how formal they are.

This problematic is also very much there on the level of housing or commoning, if you like. Practices such as kaláka, that Zsuzsi mentioned earlier, have been widespread in Eastern Europe. Thinking in strictly monetary terms, people help each other for free. But there is a moral economy to how they help each other. So, it's not objectively free: you're expected to give help back and there is a very complex system of how it is accounted for, a system that is connected at each point—in quite paradoxical and contradictory ways—to the conditions of the formal economy.

From our collective research we found that this informal aspect of the economy, and the struggle between reproductive interests and capitalist extractive interests we see in Hungary, is a generic feature of global uneven development. Its manifestations here are very similar to those in other semiperipheries. We learned that globally, people's informal reproductive work acts as a subsidy to capital from below. People reproduce themselves at least partly for free, and then are used as labor by capital.

We also see this in urban space. In urban places, especially in semiperipheries and peripheries, the incomes of a significant part of inhabitants do not cover their housing costs, and much of this gap is bridged by self-built, often informal dwellings. The research of Helyzet member András Vigvári shows this going on in Budapest's periurban areas from the 1920s, throughout socialism, until today.[4] Basically, those people work city jobs, yet reduce the cost for capital by taking care of their housing at a price that is suppressed through self-building, secondhand materials, and semilegal status. It is even more illustrative when these same people work in temporary, low-paid construction jobs on one of those overpriced inner-city real estate projects into which financialized investment is poured for speculative profit, while the workers themselves use second-hand construction materials, their free labor and skills, and the help of their peers in order to be able to live somewhere.

Our efforts to build solidarity economy solutions revolve around this question: in all aspects of the present system, there is an observable capacity of people to take care of themselves, the whole system would collapse without this massive volume of informal reproduction—how do we free this capacity from the extractive circuits of capital? This is not just a question of form, because cooperatives, just like self-built housing (two examples of what many call commoning), can be subordinated to those circuits. It is rather about tracing relations of value, trying to build technical solutions

---

4. Ágnes Gagyi and András Vigvári, "Informal Practices in Housing Financialisation: The Transformation of an Allotment Garden in Hungary," *Critical Housing Analysis* 5, no. 2 (2018): 46–55, http://www.housing-critical.com/viewfile.asp?file=2544.

that allow you to enter market relations but work against them, and building the social power that can sustain such solutions. The tricks that we are trying to think of are about how to build this capacity within conditions set in such a way that all efforts to survive are captured for profit.

Zsuzsi: Yes, I think this is the big challenge, because in the end you're using the limited resources that exist within networks, but the idea would be to draw in further resources; and not just to stretch the ones that exist already. It is always a question with these self-help structures of how much you are just cushioning the effects of a crisis or of capitalism itself. And then, when you want to draw in external resources, when you get down to the practical and technical aspects, then you realize it's not so easy to divert capital to anti-speculative and community purposes.

Ági: Although what urban movements address is very often the interface of property relations, the situation is not completely covered by the question of who owns urban real estate. What we see as this seemingly unsolvable question of urban housing poverty is ingrained in the general logic of capital reproduction, based on the capital-labor relation where labor is made free. If you look at how urbanization produces those masses "free" from their own capacity to reproduce themselves, then housing poverty has to do with the fact that while capitalism "frees" labor, it does not pay for its reproduction completely; it always generates a larger "reserve army" that is the background against which the "free" contract between labor and capital happens.

Globally, we see this in the horrible growth of slums. Even in Hungary, in a relatively good situation, there is a growing mass of people who live in cities but are unable to pay for their housing. Then there are the vertical chains through which consumption even in a Hungarian village is connected to lower positions in global labor, the effects of financialization, and lending cycles. Understanding these processes that produce urban poverty as an element of the capitalist production of space is important when thinking about urban commoning.

Mary: Ági, you recently expressed when you spoke at Luna6 that while the commons is more about property structure, the solidarity economy is about political economy and thus, more expansively "a movement to transform everything." The solidarity economy is, you said, "a technology to disrupt and transform all the means of value circulation." Can you talk a bit about the relationship between the commons and the solidarity economy?

Ági: Well, conceptually, the commons starts from an ideal scenario where the property or a certain good is collectively owned and managed. When we find these very small examples of commons, and study them up close, then we find that they have commons qualities and non-commons qualities, because of course they are still connected to the broader capitalist context. The solidarity economy perspective is not so much about identifying the qualities of this ideal situation of the commons and trying to grasp them, although this is also important because if you're not able to see it, then you can't think about potentials. Solidarity economy thinking is more about expansion, about the process: how do you go against the value circulation that now subordinates reproduction to capital extraction and what kinds of techniques, what kinds of institutions, what kinds of alternative circuits can you build? And how do you expand them against the resistance of the system?

Let's translate it to the case of urban commons. If you approach urban commons in terms of how a building can be owned and managed by a group of people, then the solidarity economy perspective would ask this: what else do these people live from? How is the building connected to utility markets or to the future pressures of selling it for a higher price? How does your institution create a capacity to go against those pressures? This is because it starts from seeing capitalism as a broad structure of capital-labor relations and real estate, housing, as one of its aspects.

Mary: So, it's expansive in the sense that it networks all these different questions about how capitalism works, and theoretically, how to transform beyond capitalism.

Ági: Yes, theoretically, and very practically. Like, we are facing climate change, right? Even if you own a building, what are you going to do with it in order to be able to resist the 40-degree heat [104°F]? How are you going to build it? From what materials? How do you get the money that you use to buy the materials? I mean it's just there in all directions.

Zsuzsi: It's also expansive in the sense that it needs to expand in order to survive. As long as these initiatives are isolated and small it's rather natural or necessary that they will be very much linked to the initiative of certain individuals or certain groups, and that they dissolve after this individual incentive is lost. I think the only way that these initiatives can become significant beyond the creation of specific spaces is if they are capable of growing, expanding, and networking. Otherwise, they just crumble under the system or dissolve into it.

Mary: In *Omnia Sunt Communia*, Massimo de Angelis writes that commons and commoning will collide with outside social systems and argues for the cultivation of a semipermeable membrane that allows for autonomy and resilience in the face of the pressures from this broader environment.[5] Can you talk about what you've been learning from this long-term praxis regarding methods that allow for a common support space, but limit how the outside effects it?

Ági: Well, it seems to me that we were working with this problem before we learned about this notion, but we really liked it, because it applies to the problematic that we're working with, and it makes it very easy to explain through real examples. One example the Peer2Peer Foundation people like to highlight is the issue of licensing. If you are open source to everyone, like Linux, then a corporation like IBM can use it as well as the community who develops it for free. But if you create a commons license that creates a membrane between commons use (for free) and market use (for pay), then you can initiate a one-way flow that can benefit the commons. In this case, the commons license would function as a semipermeable membrane. I think the alternative real estate developer has such a logic, but Zsuzsi can explain that better.

Zsuzsi: In the case of housing there are two very important instances of the semipermeable membrane. The first is when you draw in capital. We struggle a lot with the fact that you need to use resources from the markets due to the fact that real estate costs a lot of money. In this period of

5. Massimo de Angelis, *Omnia Sunt Communia: On the Commons and the Transformation to Postcapitalism* (London: Zed Books, 2017), 274.

financialization, there's so much capital going into real estate.[6] Our aim is to figure out how to create institutions able to use at least part of this capital for the purposes of the solidarity economy. The next instance is in assuring that these houses are not resold; that they are kept in the ecosystem and don't go back to the market at three times the price. Both instances are actually very complicated when you get down to the practical details. In the first instance, you have the question of what financial resources can be drawn into these alternative real estate projects. There are huge differences depending on where you are in the global economy. In many places in Western Europe and North America, such projects have become interesting for impact investors and ethical banks. In our region, these kinds of financial products are not available—and just like the mainstream commercial banks, these presumably ethical financial actors also consider our region to be riskier.

But the lack of institutional finance might also become an advantage in some cases. It was a very interesting learning experience for us that when we couldn't get a bank loan for our housing cooperative, we were able to finance 50 percent of the costs through direct loans from the network supporting our initiative. In the end we had no bank loans at all! It is very reassuring in the sense that there's this other network you can build on. However, it's not something that you can scale up really easily, so we will have to work on this a lot in the next period. Community finance can be an important resource, and having realized this, we want to develop peer-to-peer and community-based financial mechanisms in a more systematic way.

In terms of the second instance of the membrane, we've been thinking a lot about legal structures that prevent resale and ensure decommodification. There are solutions, but as long as we need to rely heavily on financial resources that individuals can bring into these housing projects, it is difficult to entirely cut out individual property rights, especially in the context of an ownership-dominated housing market. This is again the problem of where you get the resources from. The individual alternative for people in this context is to rely on property which will accrue a lot more value over time.

---

6. "Global real estate represents nearly 60 percent of the value of all global assets or $217 trillion USD—with residential real estate comprising $163 trillion USD or 75 percent. This represents more than twice the world's total GDP." See United Nations Human Rights Office of the High Commissioner, "Financialization of Housing," nd, https://www.ohchr.org/EN/Issues/Housing/Pages/FinancializationHousing.aspx.

With the alternative real estate developer, we are building an institution that can actively manage the semipermeable membrane in these different instances. It can be an actor that draws in financial resources for the purposes of real estate projects within networks of solidarity economy, and one that also creates a legal structure which can keep these properties off the market in the long term.

These dilemmas also reflect the different scales of how you relate to your outside environment. There is the scale of relating to broader capitalist processes and big market actors, and there's also the scale of drawing individuals into your alternative ecosystem. These can be difficult to bridge when creating structures that will bear the biggest results in twenty to thirty years. For instance, the houses we buy now will only become debt-free then. We need to gain peoples' confidence in a system that doesn't yet exist, which is hard. It needs a lot of trust. At the moment, these structures are still very small, but you already have to create rules for the long term and for a larger ecosystem.

Mary: I was thinking about what you have said, Zsuzsi, about "impact investors." I can see how that particular category of investors would be useful if they were in the region because they will invest in things that others

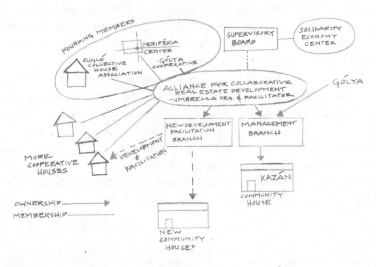

FIGURE 3.2. *Hand-drawn diagram illustrating the Gólya Cooperative's alternative real estate development. Illustration by Mary N. Taylor.*

won't, but aren't they often just as extractive? I read books on alternative investing and see authors boasting that on top of its social value it promises greater returns.

Zsuzsi: Yes, I think it's important to see that the recent interest in impact investing has also happened because there has been a general loss of profitability in many spheres. And these financial actors will not put money into anything that is risky for them or where they would not have financial gains secured. The question is whether we have any way of using these resources in a way that is acceptable for us. This is an important question in the field of housing because we will never have enough money only from our own network to acquire properties on a larger scale.

This is also where the role of the state comes in. In many contexts, less extractive financial resources available to solidarity economy-oriented real estate projects have some kind of state sponsorship. One example is subsidized loans given by public banks. This support is often given to commercial real estate actors, and only rarely to nonprofit ones. The more public money or subsidy goes into collaborative housing projects (even if this is through loans), the more affordable they can be for end users. The state can intervene in several other ways as well, from setting interest rates, through giving tax breaks, to intervening in land policy. All of these instruments influence who has an easier job on the real estate market. Sadly, I think it's to some extent an illusion that we will be able to significantly scale up these initiatives completely against both state and the market, which both have much more resources than small solidarity economy initiatives will ever have.

Mary: A strategy that community land trusts have used is to get the state to give land.

Zsuzsi: Yeah, and it's complicated, because at the same time, it is what you want to be independent from. I've been speaking to friends and colleagues from Western Europe who have had supportive state interventions before and they have said, "now we want to do a community land trust without the state and without the municipality because we've discovered that it's not good to be dependent on them." And they are now creating bottom-up land trusts that are controlled by the community organizations, aiming to fundraise for themselves from various sources.

Mary: One aspect of the relationship between commons and solidarity economies is scale. Both Periféria and the Solidarity Economy Center work primarily in the city. A lot of people speak about commoning as tiny projects, but it seems to me that when you're thinking with the solidarity economy, you can approach scale in a number of ways, also in terms of capitalist development and the way that capital works.

Ági: The Solidarity Economy Center works in Budapest. We have also been working with farmers and community-supported agriculture projects, but we are small at the moment. The most general background to this question is that we operate within this hundreds-of-years-old global system that is, you know, driving us towards catastrophe very soon and there's the real scale of that thing. Compared to that, all such initiatives look hopelessly tiny. But in thinking about the solution, you really need to consider the whole of it. That's why questions about our capacity for scaling and the question of broader value circulation are at the center, even when we are working on smaller things, and why we are not trying to develop "inspirational" models only that look good in themselves.

Zsuzsi: There's this contradiction that I mentioned earlier: it needs to grow, because otherwise it will collapse. To scale up in the field of housing, I think you need to build with or engage people who materially have a housing problem: who are having issues that are not really solved by the current conditions and for whom it is not only a political or value choice, but an economic one. At the same time, as long as we're in this difficult material position as an alternative housing network, it's actually not so accessible to people who are unable to engage with material resources and time. In order for it to keep existing, to really be able to sustain a system where these properties don't go back to the market, you need to scale up. But for that you need external resources, because building on internal ones alone is going to keep it too small and inaccessible. And being able to scale up is also very much dependent on how much you can involve other social groups, and not only the ones who would resonate with the ideology. These different elements are codependent in a way. Outside the city it's easier in many ways, since real estate prices are much lower. In our conversations with groups that want to establish rural communities that would also include agricultural activity, we are mainly able to contribute our knowledge on financial and legal aspects. But our core activities are focused in the city.

Mary: The rental housing cooperative has been looking for funds to buy property. As Zsuzsi has said, you can't compile enough resources from the solidarity economy, you have to pull in capital. What things have you learned regarding the logic of financial capital? I'm thinking about the various organizations that you've been working with or considering working with. Maybe there's a few other things that you'd like to add specifically about the logic of financial capital and also with respect to the membrane.

The membrane goes both ways, right? We cannot allow things out or we cannot allow things in, and we can selectively do both. But so many organizations that are doing initiatives that would provide cheaper housing or various kinds of access to social goods or reproductive goods, are quite attached to the logic of finance. For example, to sustain themselves and their members, cooperatives or unions may invest their funds in problematic things as they seek high rates of return. Pension funds, for example, are big investors in agricultural land grabs and commercial housing construction. The logic of finance is so pervasive—how might we interrogate these relationships?

Zsuzsi: I think that building larger networks is an important part of the answer. As long as you have an individual house or even a few houses you will be very dependent on the terms and conditions that a lender or investor will give you. We can use the example of MOBA, where the ambition is to create an internal fund that members can use and where we set the criteria and adapt it to our own needs. Of course, you need to attract money into that fund from somewhere, but then there's already this buffering institution between the financial market and the housing initiatives. And I think that this buffering function can also work on a smaller scale. For instance, what makes it worthwhile for people to go into a rental housing cooperative, rather than taking an individual mortgage? One important argument is that you're not left to face financial actors alone; there's this collective institution between them and you (but of course, many people do not have the option of taking an individual mortgage). MOBA is this protective layer on a bigger scale, and it is also a way of pulling resources into our structures. Another good example that's quite inspirational in terms of how this can expand to an international scale, is that the seed funding that we got for the MOBA revolving fund came from the biggest Swiss housing cooperative (ABZ) as a donation.

Mary: So here is the example of the Swiss cooperative acting outside of that financial logic.

Zsuzsi: Right—which they did because we have a model that is quite similar to theirs.

Ági: One more thing about the financial logic that comes down to use value. Real estate appreciation these days is a consequence of the financialization of capital during crisis. Finance capital is the most liquid form of capital but it's nothing other than capital, part of a relation the other side of which is labor, which produces capital but also needs to live somewhere. When you are building these semipermeable membrane type of institutions in terms of even already just one house, but even on higher levels like MOBA or hopefully a broad system in which you have your own bank and you circulate your own money in a different logic, there is the other side. That includes all the other functions like what you eat, where you get your heat from, how you pay for it, etc. Here lies the problem: as long as you need to work on the capitalist labor market to get those things, your whole life depends on how profitable the company in which you work can be. You need others to be exploited in order to be able to reproduce yourself, and this is why building any of these projects is not only about facing the financial logic—such as having to repay a collective loan—because you're facing the whole logic of capital relations all the time.

Mary: How can we connect commons and solidarity economy more directly to questions of debt and capitalism's compound growth rate of 3 percent? What are the ways in which the semipermeable membrane can be used not just to fund the commons but to transform relations? One of the things about the disparities of wealth at the current conjuncture is that, in order to access (even basic) resources, much less accumulate them, one of the few options people and groups have is to borrow. You're not just getting the funds but you're ending up in an often quite risky debt relationship. Insofar as capitalism as a system grows older—because the growth of global capital growth is compound—it is massively larger than it was even fifty years ago, much less two hundred years ago. I guess I'm trying to get at this question of scale as it's related to both gathering resources outside of the logic of capitalist accumulation, but also the way in which that is directly related to a compound growth rate produced mainly via finance relations, with the built environment being a big part of that. What are the ways a semipermeable membrane can be used not just to fund a commons, but to transform relations given these conditions?

Ági: Well, left analysis generally agrees that the housing problem is connected to a general problem of capitalist growth, to which financialization was supposed to produce a fix. This enhanced extractive logic is also evidenced in the financialization of agricultural land, water, and other natural resources, and the global surge of infrastructures serving long-distance financialized trade logistics, for example. The whole transformation of the labor regime over the last decades, with jobs moving to East Asia and now slowly leaving China, is part of this. Climate change and pandemic effects are by now disrupting this already extremely tight system of compensatory spatial fixes.

It's not only that capital is having a hard time recreating the conditions for its extended reproduction, but the existing channels are also breaking down. This disruption is then used as a further source of monopolization—at the top, in capitalist mergers, but at the bottom where the basic solutions for social reproduction are also being transformed into extractive targets. Just getting clean water or land where you won't have forest fires, just being able to live on one side of the border that people who are chased by bloody conflict and climate displacement are not allowed to cross. Those people who enforce that armed border control also become a source of extraction through the privatization and financialization of so-called security. This process where the conditions of bare life are becoming a source of extraction is present in the financialization of housing too. From the perspective of capital's consistent growth rate and accelerating mass, we are in a late stage of fixes to a long-term drop in profitability. Crisis disruptions are challenging the system and generating even more aggressive incursions by capital into the conditions of bare life. Of course, as we know, crises also open up cracks where reproductive aspects can be organized differently.

Zsuzsi: Regarding debt, we can also interrogate what response the solidarity economy can give to the issue. On the one hand, we can create structures of social reproduction that are not dependent on debt and allow the liberty of not entering into an individual debt relation. On the other hand, solidarity economy initiatives can also develop mechanisms that offer solutions to people who are already in a debt trap.

Mary: A lot of thinking on the commons as well as the solidarity economy, if joyfully utopian, can also be blissfully naive. On the one hand, you have the idea of commons as isolated islands, and on the other, there is the practice of naming any initiative we feel affinity with part of the solidarity economy. One of the interesting things about remaining in this kind of bliss is that it allows you not to think too critically about where the resources that you get come from. I don't want to argue that this stage of capitalism, so-called "financialization," operates differently than other stages of capitalism. What I'm interested in is how people borrow money, and insofar as you're borrowing money in a debt relationship, you're also being pulled into a particular aspect of the process of producing 3 percent compound growth because you're in debt at those rates. And yet, I hear a lot of people speaking as if that's not the case, as if they really have an autonomous sphere that's not connected to these processes at different scales.

From this perspective, I am wondering if and how degrowth could become a more useful concept for what we've been talking about here. Perhaps what I was trying to do when I formulated that question was to push you to articulate something about the imbrication of our, these, efforts into those details of capital. What happens when instead of holding up our picture of autonomy we recognize that imbrication? What happens if we recognize we are tied up in debt relations that suck resources out of our sphere to contribute to a growth that benefits extremely wealthy entities? The doubling of the wealth of billionaires across the period of the COVID-19 pandemic to date is illustrative. So, I was hoping to think creatively together about the things that jam that back, and I think you've spoken to that a bit. I mean there are these options, you know—you can get funds that aren't debt based, like seed funding. But of course, how was that money made? Is a "take the money and run" approach pretty much one of our only choices at this point? I guess other creative ways of doing it, which we haven't talked about at all here, are things like squatting or taking back municipal or private land and putting it, "property" of any kind, back towards social reproduction without the burden of debt. None of the projects we've been discussing here involve an element like that at the moment, so it makes sense that it wouldn't come up organically.

Zsuzsi: I'm happy to reflect on that, because actually, I think one of the hopes for getting financial resources for cooperative housing is that the market for individual mortgages will become saturated. This could push financial actors into new directions since they are under pressure to put their money somewhere. This can make them willing to develop new products, which we need for alternative housing projects.

However, this process pushes us into wanting to become "financially acceptable," to learn how to develop good financial plans, etc. And in a way this means we succumb to the market logic, even if we hope to be able to use it to our benefit. As opposed to that, the logic of squatting, for instance, is to take space and housing based on the fact that it is a basic necessity. What we are experimenting with is how you may take their money, and then keep it in use for our own purposes. I think that's possible, to a certain extent. That's my hope, but maybe it is naive to think that we will be outsmarting the big guys. Even in a positive scenario, yes, you are contributing to overall financial growth through the interest rates you are paying.

Ági: Maybe just one more thing to add. On the labor side, you are always producing the 3 percent. On all fronts. In all efforts to build an alternative, the question is how to build the ground on which you can extricate yourself from this, since in the given moment all of our functions are embedded in it. In terms of finance, this is a classic problem for building both cooperative systems and socialist economies because your problem is going to be that you are not getting capitalist investments. The classic solution has been to use your own resources, channel them together and then circulate them according to a different value hierarchy. This might sound good but, as we know, these systems weren't able to free themselves from the subordination to global markets, and the costs of the struggle to resist while being part of them was largely borne by the population and natural resources from which those "inner" resources were gathered.

A major cause of this, in the state socialist case, was technological dependence. To improve the terms of trade with capitalist markets, extreme efforts were made both to buy technology and produce for export at the same time—in most cases ending up in a debt crisis. The other main problem is that because these efforts imply such huge conflicts of interest most of the resources had to go to defense. Looking at these previous efforts maybe has a stronger effect on us as we are looking at them from Hungary's historical experience, so we are wary of evaluating any small initiative as the beginning of a unidirectional march towards world revolution. Even if multiple small initiatives blossom, they won't change the global system, but from where we stand, we thought we needed to do the small initiatives to even learn how this is done, what it takes, and build some social background that can exercise power towards scaling them.

Mary: What specific concerns arise when we think about urbanization and commoning in the trajectory of postsocialist and semiperipheral development in Eastern Europe? Are there things that we need to know about the region when we think about urban commoning here? The knowledge production you've been engaged in generally favors the language of semiperipheral development to that of postsocialism. It would be interesting to hear you articulate your position on this.

Zsuzsi: I guess the whole postsocialist narrative has been about catching up to capitalism, which is a different understanding of the reasons behind the social and economic conditions in these countries. The argument for using the analytics of dependency theory and world systems theory is that the current situation in these countries should not be explained by a "sidelining" of our trajectory by state socialism for forty years that we must correct so that we can return to capitalism. Rather, it can be explained by a more structural condition that takes the form of different political regimes over time. From that perspective, highlighting the state socialist period is less relevant, as it too was a specific reaction to these broader processes of uneven development.

Ági: I'll enumerate a few points we usually mention regarding how the postsocialist/semiperipheral situation affects housing struggles. Since the privatization of state socialist housing, we have a housing system characterized by *super-homeownership*, which means that the largest part of the housing stock is in the hands of private owners. This makes access to housing hard for many (as you don't have a large rental market or social housing), which is why housing-related debt is such a big issue. At the same time, this ownership system has also made it hard for large capitalist rental companies to enter the market, creating a different situation from many other places. In terms of financing, Hungary is in a subordinated position both in terms of its currency and the banking system, which appears even in how Western cooperative banks come to Eastern Europe to make higher profits. Meanwhile, cooperative financing and housing structures built up during socialism were largely canceled, so when you try to get a deal as a cooperative neither banks nor local governments get what you are talking about. MOBA came together based on the common understanding that the new cooperative initiatives in the region are in the same situation in that you don't have much rental housing and that cooperative rental housing solutions have a really hard time accessing finance.

Mary: Another question connected to trying to do cooperative projects or projects that are associated with commoning in a postsocialist context—or maybe I'll say post-Communist here—regards language. This is a context in which people have had a negative experience with something called Communist, as well as collectivist projects associated to that project, not to mention being subject to dominant liberal arguments that present it as an historical aberration, as Zsuzsi notes. What does it mean to pursue projects like this that can be coded as Communism (again, or differently) or not? I guess I'm asking about ideological openings or closures.

Zsuzsi: The common opinion is that people would refuse anything that has a similar vocabulary to institutions that existed during state socialism. But I think it's not so straightforward, and it depends a lot on the local context; on how collectivization happened in any given place, for example. It depends on the sector. Housing cooperatives, for instance, were actually a hidden way of accessing individual ownership in Hungary in the 1980s. Given this, our difficulty lies in explaining why the housing cooperatives we are promoting go against individual ownership. Agricultural cooperatives may have a different connotation, because they are often linked to violent collectivization. I prefer to reclaim these terms rather than deny them. But some groups in MOBA explicitly use a different term for housing cooperatives than what was used during state socialism, so it varies.

Mary: One of the propositions of this book is that the language of the commons and commoning offers a horizon for a different kind of communism than that associated with the state socialist regimes in Eastern Europe. It was interesting that each of you separately misread commonist as communist when I invited you to take part in this project.

When we speak to what is being called commons or commoning in this volume it seems important to articulate that this language does not really have a strong presence in the projects that you're involved in—in fact it doesn't seem to be essential at all.

Zsuzsi: It's hard to say how much this is a language problem and how much it's a conceptual one. But it's definitely important that it was the Solidarity Economy Center that started to frame this issue for us in Hungary, and they made a conscious choice to use the solidarity economy framework.

Ági: On the level of organizing, I think the best way to approach this is a practical one, taking into account who you are speaking to and what project you are trying to work on with them. It is these processes that imply some actual involvement and stakes that the concepts travel through and gain their social weight. For instance, this year we had these large popular protests in Georgia against a hydropower project that is basically privatizing the whole river. In this context, the idea that the river should not be privatized is becoming a real thing. From what I know they don't necessarily call it commons, but I see this as an example where a broader popular consciousness asserts that something is being made into a commodity that should not be one. In the whole conceptualization of the commons idea (and what it could mean legally), antiprivatization struggles around water in Italy played the same role; not only in terms of protest but also in terms of how you then build the capacity to institutionalize it. On the whole, I think this is about how the reality of the struggle is born, not so much about what state the debate about concepts is in. It is not so much the concept itself that is important, but this transformation of relations.

Mary: Early on in our conversation you described yourselves as being very interested in autonomy, but at the same time, you are situated in this dialectic of building some type of autonomy while using the state to help do that. Yet small-scale autonomy is not your end goal either, because beyond these initiatives, there's the question of producing a larger scale of interaction or provisioning, if you will. Perhaps you would want to speak to that: the state as a tool, end goal, or horizon?

Zsuzsi: It's a difficult question. It would be good to use the state as a tool but in the current Hungarian context it is not a realistic possibility that we would be able to use the central state in any way. In many cases (in other countries), collaborative housing projects are currently supported by the local state. In Hungary, however, local municipalities have very limited resources, partly due to the Fidesz government's strategy to starve out the local liberal-left governments. Socially sensitive municipalities will often choose to use these very limited resources—rightfully!—to improve the housing situation of the most vulnerable social groups or for groups they find to be most important in their own constituency. The housing of these groups could perhaps be served by housing cooperatives, but from the perspective of the municipality it would be more complicated than plain rental housing. Finally, these models are still difficult to understand for local state actors who have no experience with them and tend to associate cooperatives with state socialism. Thus, cooperative housing initiatives will not have access to these resources under the current conditions in Hungary.

Ági: Regarding the state as a tool or end goal, even if we are doing small initiatives and simultaneously thinking about the broader dialectics between state and movement that doesn't mean that we actually have influence on them. There is no class-based political capacity from below in Hungary right now.

What is called official politics today in Hungary basically operates on a middle-class and upper-middle-class basis, while special pockets of society are penetrated by the electoral machine for specific purposes. This is a blunt or even boring reality but it's something that has to be mentioned whenever we speak about possible relations between anticapitalist struggle and formal politics. If you go into representative politics today, under the present circumstances you'll have close to zero connection with the people whose interests you want to represent, other than symbolic messaging, which might get you some parliamentary seats but won't give you power in closed meetings with capitalist lobbies who hold social power. International left circles have been having these debates after the UK's [Jeremy] Corbyn and the US' [Bernie] Sanders campaigns failed, so I don't want to repeat these points—but the main idea is that electoral struggle is necessary, but without social power it is toothless, and you cannot build social power through the type of organizing that is formed through electoral campaigns.

Seeing the aftermath of the 2008 financial crisis in Hungary, we wanted to go into economic projects because we saw that this work was necessary but tended to be neglected here by the successive mobilizations around neoliberal crisis measures, and later, around Fidesz's new illiberal authoritarianism. These have sometimes included references to social issues but have mostly revolved around fast electoral coalitions with bourgeois opposition parties. In this context, our first attempts at collaborations that allow the next step in scaling up are focused instead on unions and local governments. On our present level, our next step towards the broader "political dialectics" are collaborations with unions where we link rank-and-file organizing with solidarity economy solutions.

Mary: For many, the language of commoning codes with autonomy from both capital and the state. Can you speak about your approaches to commoning and solidarity economy from the perspective of the state, autonomy, and/or dual power?

Zsuzsi: Just on a very pragmatic level, I think the solidarity economy approach to organize people according to their material needs can be a powerful way to build a social basis for social power. But then again there's the contradiction that as long as you're small it's hard to convince people that you're actually going to be able to respond to these material needs.

Ági: I think we still haven't come up with a better strategy than the classic strategy of dual power, meaning that you need power to make the rules, yet the effectivity of those rules relies not in the state administrative structure, but in the social power that is embedded in the whole organization of society. You do need to implement those rules within the state administration too, but to have that, you need power within the real economy, within the structures of social reproduction. In the classic dual power model, this would be the role of the *soviets* [councils], the form where labor holds power within social reproduction.

Chapter 4

RECLAIMING CARE IN THE URBAN COMMONS

CareNotes Collective

In New York City, the COVID-19 pandemic has intensified conversations around healthcare, care work, and reproducing care in common. As capital's crises intensify and quicken, we face a moment of flux—of imminent uncertainty and possibility which inspires thought and action toward reclaiming care work on the horizon of the urban commons.

Care Work beyond Capitalism

In our investigation *For Health Autonomy*—which explored the incredible visions, energies, and practices unfolding in the context of autonomous health clinics in Greece during times of austerity—our focus of concern, which is continued here, was those practices of care that have so often been institutionalized as "healthcare," (re)producing a boundary between professionals and other givers of care based on certifications and expertise, often reifying these relations into a service that someone must pay for. [1] We pointed out that capitalist institutions organizing healthcare are desperate to discover new diseases—whether to sell commodities like drugs, surgical supplies, and medical interventions or to gain property rights. Endeavoring to deinstitutionalize healthcare, we will write "health/care" here to illustrate

---

1. See CareNotes Collective, *For Health Autonomy* (Brooklyn: Common Notions, 2020).

the problem of institutions and their role in individualizing and pacifying a potentially militant exploited public.

How do we deinstitutionalize health/care as part of reclaiming care toward the horizon of the urban commons? With many companerxs around the world, we believe that the sphere of social reproduction is central to the ways we can common "against and beyond capitalism." We thus begin with some thoughts on "care" and "care work" in terms of social reproduction and the reproduction of collectivities. To us, "reproductive work" refers to all those activities and practices that contribute to the reproduction of human beings, and therefore, the commodity which is labor power. Whether waged or unwaged, whether childcare or elder care, housework or sex work, reproductive work is labor.[2] While this work contributes to the social reproduction of the worker at reduced cost for capital, it is also the work that reproduces our collective life.

As Silvia Federici writes, "The commoning of reproductive activities, at all levels, is very important to guarantee survival and to not depend completely on the market and the state for our reproduction."[3] Struggles around reproduction and care are therefore the basis for building our desire for the common. Our new society will have to be capable of reproducing itself, building from collective struggles around land, food, water, and health. This means that we must collectively restore the waters and the land of our planet "to communal use against historic and ongoing colonial and capitalist enclosures."[4]

Although movements led by domestic workers have sometimes used "care work" to create a distinction from the tasks that they are responsible for with regard to employers, we treat care work as a domain that also includes much of this labor. This is because "the 'care,' affection and relationality required to look after a child or sick person" can't be separated or made discrete from the various tasks that include washing them, folding

---

2. Camille Barbagallo and Silvia Federici, "Introduction: Care Work and the Commons," *The Commoner* 15 (Winter 2012).

3. Silvia Federici, "The Common is Us," in *For Health Autonomy*, ed. CareNotes Collective (Brooklyn: Common Notions, 2020), 14.

4. Federici, "The Common is Us," 13.

their clothes, or cleaning the places where they rest or play.[5] "Care work" illustrates the impossibility of separating immaterial from material labor.[6] Using care work in this wider sense helps us to make visible to ourselves the transversal connections across seemingly different domains of reproductive work that animate the complex dynamics and relations of urban commoning.[7]

In this vision, care work includes cleaning, shopping, cooking, doing the laundry, and paying bills. It includes provision of intimacy and emotional support. It includes bearing and raising children. It includes all the labor that goes into anticipating, preventing, and resolving crises, sustaining relations with our neighbors and kin. It includes all the hours of fetching fuel, water, and food, of providing company, and of sex work.[8] It includes the labor of keeping ourselves, one another, and our collectives healthy, physically, mentally, and spiritually. It also includes caring for the land and water that keep us alive.

---

5. Barbagallo and Federici, "Carework and the Commons," 15.

6. Barbagallo and Federici, "Carework and the Commons," 15.

7. Guattari's concern with the institution connects with the later period of writing with Deleuze, in which he continued to develop his understanding of transversality. However, Guattari was already exploring transversality "a concept that seeks directly to transform institutional realities by shifting the way in which people produce themselves and their relations to others within institutions" in the 1960s. This involved experiment with group practice within psychiatric institutions to generate analytic effects regarding the circulation of desire, and the production of subjectivities. See Félix Guattari, *Psychoanalysis and Transversality: Texts and Interviews 1955–1971*, trans. Ames Hodges (Los Angeles: Semiotext(e), 2015), 110; Andrew Goffey, "Guattari and Transversality: Institutions, Analysis and Experimentation," *Radical Philosophy* (January–February 2016): 38–47.

Guattari used transversality as a method to experiment with collective practices that "worked across the confines of the institution itself." It is a more broadly relevant tool for opening closed logics and the hierarchical ascription of identities by experimenting with relations of interdependency to produce new assemblages and alliances across institutions and beyond them. The transversal is the production of subjectivity (or the social subject) and the self-engendering practices that seek to create their own signifiers and systems of value. As Susan Kelly writes: "Forms of alliance that are appropriate to their collective actions . . . cannot leave intact the fields that they have worked across." Transversality, as temporary organization and alliance that is continuously constituted, ruptures "inherited forms of political organization that create institutional objects." See Kelly, "The Transversal and the Invisible: How do you really make a work of art that is not a work of art?" *Transversal* (January 2005), https://transversal.at/transversal/0303/kelly/en.

8. Barbagallo and Federici, "Carework and the Commons," 15.

Reclaiming Care in Urban Commons

The COVID-19 pandemic has intensified our conversations around healthcare, care work, and reproducing care in common. In New York City, from where we write, many care workers, mostly women of color, have died while staffing hospitals, nursing homes, and supermarkets that seldom serve their own communities. Protests led by healthcare workers, teachers, transit workers, laundry workers, and other care workers have challenged the "business as usual" that threatens their lives. Mutual aid networks emerged across the city to help neighbors with food, health/care, and other needs. Social centers, churches, and car services provided food on a large scale from their collective spaces, and an antigentrification group built a network of callers and deliverers to check in and provide for neighbors on the scale of an entire borough.

Community gardens experimented with new ways of cultivating and sharing food with neighbors and produced remedies from medicinal plants, while composting and gardening enhanced gardeners' microbiomes. A city-wide network of community refrigerators made and supported relations between previously unconnected places and people, just as CSAs have more deeply woven us together with our bioregion. Similar efforts multiplied in many forms, and people met with many others to ask the "what, how, and why" of general strike while unfurling rent strike banners from windows. By Summer 2020, our city, among many others, rose up against police killings: Black Lives Matter flags flew high.

Alongside these inspiring events, police killings, evictions, hospital closures and understaffing, and other modes of capitalist and state violence are accelerating processes of selective enclosure, primarily in communities of color. The scale of violence demands strategies beyond singular struggles and care practices, and insights beyond academic abstractions of care. The commons and the problematic of its reproduction arise as an urgent collective conversation rooted in our current conditions of precarization. This conversation is set upon rupturing the "I" towards a horizon of the "we," in practice and in knowledge production, to invoke a material and spiritual rupture from the parallel processes of the "I"nstitutionalization and financialization of our care practices.[9] This rupture, towards a horizon of the reproduction of "our" commons, acknowledges the reproduction of our bodies and ecologies through rhizomatic, interdependent, and expansive relations crucial for sustaining the very existence of our various struggles.

But how can we engage in a transversal reproduction of the commons, beyond the existing capitalist institutions and territorialized activist practices around care?[10] What modes of knowledge production are emerging rhizomatically in the context of urban struggles around housing, healthcare, elder care, community farms, prison abolition, and other movements toward reproducing care? In this context of violence and dispossession, understanding how to recuperate minds, bodies, and ecologies to transform not only the material possibilities around the commons but its affective or spiritual field of consciousness is critical.

---

9. "I"—the individual—is an institutionalization which prevents us from recognizing our relationalities and our communal condition. Capitalist institutionalization of care practices shapes this "I" in contract to the "we" or "ours." Our use of the term institutionalization and its variant "I"nstitutionalization" derives from the work of Félix Guattari and emerged in the context of his experience as a psychiatrist, hospital worker, and clinician taking part in the antipsychiatry movement. Guattari's critique of the individual, colleague, citizen, and the philosophy of "methodological individualism" at the core of clinical analysis and the consulting room relates to his broader concern with "institutionalization" as the "problem of the production of institutions." Exploring the problematic of desire and of subjectivity, individual and collective, Guattari asks, "who produces the institution and articulates its sub-groups? Is there a way to modify this production?" See Guattari, *Psychoanalysis and Transversality*, 62.

In relation to his experience of the institutionalization of social movement activity in 1968, Guattari suggested that "the institution is the 'unit of production' of subjectivity" (see Goffey, "Guattari and Transversality"). When we write "I"nstitutionalization we highlight Guattari's concern that "the general proliferation of institutions in contemporary society leads only to reinforcing the alienation of the individual." Guattari distinguishes between subject groups and those who are subjugated, that "receive the law" or we can say identity, "from outside," and asks: "is it possible to operate a transfer of responsibility, replacing bureaucracy with institutional creativity? See Guattari, *Psychoanalysis and Transversality*, 62.

10. Each assemblage or institution is territorial/territorialized, and rupturing it or moving beyond it to the outside constituted through its boundary, deterritorialization must take place. While capitalism tends to reterritorialize (and here despite the philosophical distance, we might see a trace of Marx's fetish), deterritorialization comes about via lines of flight, one category of "desire lines" that Deleuze and Guattari present for breaking away from prescribed patterns. See Joshua Windsor, "Desire Lines: Deleuze and Guattari on Molar Lines, Molecular Lines, and Lines of Flight," *New Zealand Sociology* 30, no. 1 (2015): 157; Gilles Deleuze and Félix Guattari, *Anti-Oedipus: Capitalism and Schizophrenia*, trans. Robert Hurley, Mark Seem, and Helen Lane (New York: Penguin Group, 1977). Lines of flight neither follow scripted pathways nor do they have a scripted destination. As desire lines, they are movements of radical becoming. Rather than flights from, they are lines that transform the context itself. While transversality explicitly sets out to deterritorialize the institutions, fields, and significations it works across, reterritorialization is common. We can say that deterritorialization means multiple moves toward the changing horizon.

Care Work as Integral to Reproducing the Commons

The material realities around sustaining life in our urban context rely on extractivism for obtaining food, fresh water, medicines, and fuel. Migrant workers grow most of the food produced in our country. Women of color bear the burden of caring for children, elders, and patients. Workers of color rush to low-wage service jobs, to fill shelves, cook, deliver dinners, and wash our laundry. Care workers have long been exposed to the most harrowing conditions to satisfy our individualized needs.

This reality was highlighted with the pandemic as cities panicked over supplies of food and medicines, and workers were rushed to work at farms, supermarkets, and hospitals, and to perform other essential tasks without even the most basic protections. Although efforts to mobilize around rent strikes, general strike, prison abolition, and mutual aid networks following the onset of the pandemic are important and inspiring, past and present experiences in reproducing care in common highlight the need to mobilize across separate struggles to meet our needs at the scale of an entire community, or even the entire city. Our capacity to envision a particular mobilization as interdependent with other struggles is absolutely critical. It is also a cornerstone for, and an initial glimpse of, a reproduction of the commons that is self-sufficient and reduces the toll on our ecologies and care workers.

Imagine networks of community farms and rooftop gardens cultivating herbal remedies and foods that nourish rent strikers, who are then able to liberate more abandoned rooftops and empty lots to seed the next wave of community farms! The interdependence between bodies freed from rent or prisons capable of farming, feeding, and healing is inspiring. It also requires a scale able to offset our extractivist existence in urban spaces. This means that while local disaster-response mutual aid efforts are crucial, we must move toward a horizon that is capable of sustaining cities through interdependent networks of organizations indefinitely. At this scale, we can already imagine how we relate with ecologies beyond the city limits. By linking our urban contexts into their bioregions and recuperating our ecosystems through reforestation and permaculture in the Global North, we reduce demand for food and energy extracted from the Global South. Our consumption becomes linked to our contexts. Through this process, we can move to reduce the devastating impact of global warming, pandemics, hurricanes, and other "natural" disasters on our bodies, communities, and ecosystems.

Restoring and Restorative Care beyond the Individual

The pandemic has also crystallized the consequences of the near absence of common knowledges, practices, and spaces capable of preventing infection and the spread of disease, as well as responding to the symptoms of COVID-19. Here, we can grasp the importance of sustained and collective learning and experience with restorative remedies, such as herbal, fungal, nutritional, and meditation practices. Many of these restorative practices emphasize a preventative approach to health that nurtures the body's innate potential to mitigate the impact of infections and physical or emotional distress. Learning them, we can also avoid a "disaster response" mentality that risks immersing our collectives in reactive, acute, and even militaristic relations around providing care.

In such moments, when a disaster response is stoked, it is hard to take time to discuss the ramifications of how care is organized or to dwell on questions about our capacity to challenge escalating capitalist dispossession. Approaches to restorative care as a practice of community-building may be cast aside, and disaster responses may trigger microfascisms, through internalization of roles such as "savior" and "victim," alienating potentialities for reproducing the commons collectively. Learning practices of slow care within, against, and beyond the temporalities of disaster response in conditions of escalating capitalist dispossession is a challenge that we must take up. This means learning new habits of relating and communication that function on a different temporality than much of the immediate action that our context demands from us.

These habits can help us deterritorialize identities promoted by the healthcare system that affect our understanding of individual and collective suffering. While identification with a diagnosis can lead to collective experiences, for example in group meetings, it can contribute to notions of suffering that obscure our relationalities with care workers and others experiencing myriad forms of suffering. When we resist internalizing diagnoses imposed by the biomedical model we open ourselves up to seeing the political, economic, and ecological forces that triggered so much of this suffering. We open connections between our suffering and that of striking healthcare workers, teachers, laundry and Amazon and Starbucks workers, who we might otherwise be tempted to blame for not meeting our needs, especially when we are ill or under stress. We open pathways to reproducing care in common.

Beyond the Binary of the Biomedical Model vs. Restorative Care

Resisting the internalization of such categories means not clinging to a binary between the biomedical model and restorative practices. This would simply entrench how we define care in ways detrimental to our bodies and divisive when working to collectivize around care. Most anyone who has committed to caring for elders, children, or a loved one with a chronic disease realizes the importance of access to effective biomedical care. In New York and other cities, some people in anticapitalist spaces may consider hospital or clinic closures a success, without comprehending that such closures are centered in working class neighborhoods and communities of color and can offer so much critical space for care work.

The example of the struggles led by the Young Lords at Lincoln Hospital (in the South Bronx in 1970, in cooperation with the Black Panthers and health/care workers)—from the liberation and recuperation of hospital space and medical vehicles to the implementation of programs oriented toward mental health, addiction, and general care—shows that it is possible to turn hospital space, resources and personnel toward "people's programs" of care in our own city.[11] The Zapatistas have also shown that in Chiapas, developing knowledge via "health promoters" can channel preventative and restorative practices through communities that lessen, but do not eliminate, the need for hospitals.[12]

The point of our struggle is not to dehospitalize our urban spaces and neglect them for developers and speculation, but to de-"I"nstitutionalize the hospitals and clinics that remain to provide forms of biomedical or restorative care, and many of the other things required for our common survival and the cultivation of our commons beyond capitalism. Imagine endless lobbies and auditoriums for teach-ins and assemblies; rooftops and parking lots for *refarming* and horticultural therapy; and walls for murals and vertical gardens for our herbal remedies! Picture teach-ins on various

---

11. See Woodbine.NYC, *Fight Like Hell for the Living: A Health Autonomy Reader* (2017), 26–40; *Health/PAC Bulletin* 37 (January 1972); the documentary film *Takeover: How We Occupied a Hospital and Changed Public Healthcare*, dir. Emma Francis-Snyder, 2021, 38 minutes.
12. Woodbine.NYC, *Fight Like Hell*, 41–45.

health conditions or care practices, support group meetings, emergency housing and support for women surviving physical and sexual violence, open kitchens, recording studios disseminating liberated knowledges and experiences! Restorative remedies, practices and teachings, typically for sale in more affluent neighborhoods, can be liberated for the entire city through their cultivation across community farms and fire escape gardens, study groups, and apartment kitchens; strengthening our physical and mental health through access to microbiomes in the living soil and the joy of connecting to plants, the earth, and one another.

From Liberating Healthcare Spaces to a Deterritorialized State of Care

The extent to which we are able to imagine health/care practices beyond the limits of hospital, clinic, meditation retreat, or sweat lodge and relate them to a broader reproduction of the commons is critical. For those of us working as healers and/or teachers, the questions include, how can we be gradually peripheralized within a group as knowledge is being liberated? To what extent are we able to move beyond treatment, prevention, and self-care to embrace liberated housing, open kitchens, community farms, and collective dinners as transformative care? How can we unfold transformative practices in their capacity to liberate everyday life, spaces, and relations, and prevent the re-institutionalization of roles, experts, and "working groups" that limit our collective capacity to reproduce care collectively?

Given institutionalized and internalized roles, expertise, and affects, reproducing care collectively is a challenge and requires us to imagine new sensibilities and techniques to liberate care practices. But where do we start? In the clinic, kitchen, or parks? In the virtual world? In all these places? The answer depends on what precarities are afflicting our bodies or ecosystems, the means we have to gather and discuss the(se) issue(s) with others, and our capacity to explore spaces and practices that could amplify desires of reproducing care in common.

As the pandemic continues, many clinics and hospitals in New York City face severe budget cuts. Suicides and COVID-19 deaths plague healthcare workers, while large tech companies are finding lucrative opportunities to penetrate remote health platforms (e.g., telemedicine, wearable devices, home medication deliveries) and our everyday lives. These same workers—however, especially nurses—have been the most politicized and prolific in resisting hospital closures and layoffs, while demanding universal testing and vaccinations, and mobilizing against "business as usual" to protect the millions of other care workers that sustain urban life. Rank-and-file healthcare workers have seen their coworkers and countless patients die, while enduring constant intimidation from their union and hospital bosses. Yet they have sought to unite their struggle with other care workers, including teachers, Amazon workers, and transit workers.

This momentum, mostly driven by nurses, has the potential to link with other community and city-wide initiatives relevant to our struggle around reproducing the commons to demand worker and community-run clinics, hospitals, and health departments. With the absence of profit-driven bosses, we can experiment with participatory budgeting, consensus-based decision making, and collective learning in improving various aspects of care. We can convert office space once belonging to bosses to be used for mutual aid group meetings, teach-ins on biomedical and restorative remedies, and greenhouses for cultivating herbal and fungal remedies. In such a moment, we can finally realize the desire towards de-institutionalization rather than de-hospitalization.

The lessons we have learned from the Black Panthers and Young Lords highlight possibilities of empowering ourselves during times of physical, emotional, and community level distress to organize mutual aid and support group formations, sharing resources and experiences for coping and recovering, organizing teach-ins around health conditions and remedies, accompanying friends to clinic visits as their advocates, and encouraging caregivers to form support networks. The purpose of such formations is not to antagonize health/care workers but rather to empower ourselves to navigate around our health needs, have our questions and concerns addressed, and provide additional support for our loved ones after a doctor's visit.

Imagining Care Work beyond the Clinic

There are many limitations to enacting what we have proposed here in New York City, a city dominated by real estate values. Yet, numerous examples around the globe highlight the inspiring experiences related to social clinics, social spaces for health, and other practices that reorganize space to facilitate the collectivization of care with assemblies, teach-ins, and mutual aid groups; while clinicians, medications, and herbal remedies are located more peripherally in the space. These possibilities for liberating space beyond the clinic inspire us to imagine how community centers, parks, laundromats, subway stations, or workplaces could be transformed for healing versus productivity. In Greece, the Workers' Health Center at the self-managed VIOME factory in Thessaloniki offers an inspiring model for how clinical care can be integrated in a factory space. It takes a holistic approach, in which the intake team is made up of "healthcare experts" and "nonexpert" community members together in order to embrace an individual's emotional, physical, and economic needs.

But what if an entire plaza, complex of buildings, neighborhood, or territory were recuperated towards a sphere of non-capitalist life and reproducing care? In Athens, the Exarchia neighborhood has been able to reproduce itself as a commons around an amalgamation of liberated housing, open kitchens, community gardening, film screenings, a social clinic, and organized defense against police raids, the mafia, and neo-Nazis to ensure a safe space for so many migrants and Greeks. It is reproducing a commons partially autonomous from capitalist life. The Zapatistas have shown us anticapitalist reproduction on the scale of a territory, built through resistance and by building across *caracol* communities, with health promoters offering a specific example of territory wide health/care practice.

There is a long road ahead, yet actively imagining this urban commonist horizon is essential. We have shared with you some of the valuable collective activities animating our city and the immanent possibilities we see in the time of COVID-19. Walking toward a common horizon we must keep asking questions. For instance, how do we move towards making our care practices more and more part of everyday life? To what extent are we reproducing collective knowledge rather than a new generation of experts? How can we organize to collectively learn basic healing practices using meditation, and biomedical, herbal, fungal, and nutritional remedies, while collaborating with an "expert" when facing circumstances too complex for us? How can we recuperate more spaces of many kinds, from abandoned buildings and lots, parks, laundromats, independent pharmacies, or schools, where so much space and time is available beyond usual operating hours? Joining with people who inhabit those spaces to facilitate neighborhood-led practices reproducing care, we can link these efforts across the city and into our bioregion. Finally, we need to follow paths to embracing a spiritual connection to our practices. How such a connection is experienced will vary by context and culture but must be held against so much of the violence and psychosis of urban capitalist life.

Chapter 5

CAPITAL'S SOCIAL FIX: DIVESTMENT AND AGENCY IN THE POST-SOCIALIST REGENERATE CITY

Naujininkai Commons Collective (Vaiva Aglinskas, Vaida Stepanovaitė, and Noah Brehmer)

At a community-organized meeting to discuss "Vilnius Connect"¹—a multimillion-euro development plan targeting the heavily stigmatized and financially divested working-class district Naujininkai—the large school hall was almost full despite Lithuanian Railways and Vilnius Connect having organized its own presentation just two days before, in what seemed like a scrambled effort to officially publicize plans before the community exposed them. A lively discussion followed the presentations and panelists' conversations in which residents voiced their concerns about inconveniences caused by a decade of construction works; the increased traffic, air, and sound pollution; and the city's prioritization of developers' access and zoning needs over the social needs of residents. They were countered by a real estate developer in the audience, explaining to them that the value of their property will increase, and that they could only stand to benefit from the surrounding investments into the neighborhood because the prices of their homes will increase. His logic, placing all importance on the exchange value of real estate, clashed with the use-value arguments of the residents who

---

1. The first stages of this developer-directed and municipality-backed gentrification plan had already begun by 2021. Their goal is to incorporate the microdistrict into the commercial flows of the city center, which it is adjacent to, through the long-term leasing of municipal land alongside the railway for commercial developments; commissioning a new railway station complex by Zaha Hadid Architects; and investment in urban infrastructure, with small parks, bike paths, and other amenities to attract the district's "future" higher-net-worth residents.

were not as concerned about making a profit as they were anxious about having to move because the quality of their surroundings and lives would become intolerable.

After the public meeting, organizers from a community group opposing the developments—the Naujininkai Initiative Group—gathered at a flat in a building near the tracks where several members live. They chatted together on the fourth-story balcony inside the courtyard, overlooking an outside stairwell built along several stories of storage sheds and tomato plants growing in DIY planters along the railing. Sounds of railway announcements periodically drifted over conversations about the successful turnout to the meeting, problematic dynamics among neighbors, and the uncertainty that the new Vilnius Connect development plans cast on the host's own plans and efforts to renovate their apartment. Was it even worth it?

I left this party after dark, and as I walked toward the old town, a middle-aged man on crutches came out from the shadows of the railway overpass. His one foot was completely twisted so that he was stepping on his ankle. There was a large plastic shopping bag on the ground next to him. As I approached, he asked me if I can help him carry it. I said of course. "You can put it just over there, on the bench by the trees." He pointed to a dimly lit park across the street. I suggested I'd walk with him there, as I was in no hurry. "Do you live around here?" I asked. "I sleep outside," he replied.

Somewhere near the crosswalk we switched over to Russian, and he told me how he used to work in construction making nine hundred euros a month, and that now he only receives fifty. His wife had left him. Recently he had been living with his current partner in a squatted basement in Naujininkai, but they got kicked out of there when they found a lock put on the door. Now they usually sleep on a forested hillside behind a bus stop up the road. Tonight, he was probably going to stay on this bench instead of trekking up there with the grocery bag. I offered to bring him a blanket, but he refused saying they need a tent more than a blanket, or better yet, he asked me to keep my eyes peeled for a shed or a basement in the area that was unlocked. I could find him most days sitting in the park, in front of the Gates of Dawn, if I were to come upon one.

Suddenly I found myself in the position of a "real estate agent" being asked to operate according to very different logics than those of the developer who spoke at the meeting earlier that evening. Taking the standpoint of my new client, I came to wonder if there could, in fact, be another path for the district's future,

*one that would break from a logic that values profitability over use and private
possession over common inhabitation? What would it mean to "speculate" on
this future from the standpoint of the underhoused, the precarious, the ethnically and socially marginalized who currently reside in this neighborhood?*

*A conversation soon transpired at a community-organized social center in
the district, Luna6, that would eventually lead to the formation of the militant
research group Naujininkai Commons. And so, setting up operations at Luna6,
our research practice has since come to take multivalent form as a transnational
dialogue with other urban thinkers and activists, district community meals,
workshops, and counter-mapping practices.[2]*

In this chapter, we offer a provisional strategy for the constitution of an
urban commons, extending from immediate struggles faced in our neighborhood to a city-wide and even global thrust for commonism as a real alternative to the capitalist world system. We begin this inquiry with an expansive
historical exploration of commoning practices in Vilnius since the 1990s.
Searching for strategies that could wager long-term and scaled-up victories
over capitalist urbanization processes, we investigate the shifting composition between divestment, social crisis or abandonment, the agential formations engendered by these processes, and the corresponding governance
models that contain them. Reflecting on the changing compositions of
these agencies, we propose the concept of *divested agency* as a way of understanding the historical specificity of commoning as mediated by changing
compositions of capital and state: the lines between legality and illegality;
permissible and impermissible; formal and illicit.

As you will see in the historical mapping of divested agency that follows, the importance of specificity in its strategic capacity to show why
what may have worked in the past is no longer sufficient as a point of antagonism and insurgency in the present. As we will demonstrate, the refractory, antagonistic social claims to urban space made by yesterday's divested
agents have been systematically incorporated into governance strategies as
a "social fix" for today's reproductive crisis. This includes outsourcing the
costs of asset maintenance and social reproduction onto communities and
temporarily displacing the social antagonisms that come with the general

---

2. This account is the recollection of an individual Naujininkai Commons member, discussing
the formation of the group at Luna6.

onslaught of for-profit development futures that are engendered by capital's ruthless drive for profit.

We conclude our analysis by returning to our starting point for this edited collection—the Naujininkai district and Luna6—taking a first step towards the commonist horizon by mapping possible solidarities between emerging commonist formations within and adjacent to our district. We address how what Stavros Stavrides refers to as *thresholds* could be cultivated between enclaves.[3] We consider the possibility of thresholding between the three enclaves profiled in this chapter—a migrant detention center, the nongovernmental organization Vilnius Social Club, and the cultural complex SODAS 2123—to both achieve the immediate need of unenclosing one (the migrant detention center) and for the long-term goal of building a culture and economy of solidarity between the many other groups, spaces, and organizations in and beyond the city. It is only from the practical building of solidarity through thresholds that these enclaves will individually be able to defend themselves from the development futures looming in their respective futures. In conclusion, we rehearse a speculative scenario wherein divested agents from enclaves across the city would unite in a movement for the constitution of public-common partnerships: a transitory tool on the way to commonism allowing for direct, democratic control over the distribution of value that does not rely on the nationalization and centralization of private enterprise.

Collapse, Criminality, and Commoning

> State run control mechanisms have been destroyed, and their replacement with new ones has only started. Anarchy in the economy is accompanied by the moral and ethical deformation of the state.
> —Anu Leps, *A Crime Forecast for Estonia*, 1994

> The law locks up the man or woman
> Who steals the goose from off the common,

---

3. As Stavrides comments, "Rather than perpetuating an image of this city as an archipelago of enclave islands, we need to create spaces that inventively threaten this peculiar urban order by upsetting dominant taxonomies of spaces and life types. Spaces-as-thresholds acquire a dubious, precarious perhaps but also virus-like existence: they become active catalysts in processes of reappropriating the city as commons." See Stavros Stavrides, *Common Space: The City as Commons* (London: Zed Books, London: 2016), 56.

But lets the greater villain loose
Who steals the common from the goose.
—Anonymous English Proverb[4]

While the new enclosures that unfolded in the West from the seventies on had parallel histories in the Soviet Union (international loans and austerity policies already accruing from 1973), Lithuania, and other former Soviet republics, experienced a hyper-accelerated neoliberal restructuring drive after independence in 1991. The privatization process was rapid. It was organized through a system of state-distributed vouchers which functioned as a kind of currency for the private appropriation of flats, land, or joint-stock holdings in companies (97.2 percent of Lithuania's housing stock was privatized through the voucher system by 1994).[5] Working-class Lithuanians who managed to attain vouchers were exposed to the perils of deregulated financial risk in the new predatory market economy, often losing their holdings by way of evictions, forced sale of flats, pyramid schemes, and the bankruptcy of joint-stock enterprises. A vicious deterioration of living standards appeared in unprecedented rates of unemployment, withdrawal of social welfare, the widespread enclosure of social infrastructure through private appropriation, and its dispossession by way of financialized accumulation.

Unlike Western paths of neoliberal governmentality that have secured capital's new enclosures through the expansion of the state's military and policing apparatus, neoliberalism in the ex-Soviet Bloc unfolded as a more encompassing *de*formation of state. In Lithuania, a dual movement of desecuritization (14,000 state security or "extra-departmental militia" were laid off in 1991 alone) and privatization offered fertile ground for the rise of both clandestine and illicit organizations, such as the "higher" criminals of the new ruling class and the working-class commoning movements.[6] These agential formations, emerging out of conditions of divestment, articulated their claims through new and unfamiliar forms of social agency. It was an agency born out of divestment: divested agency.

---

4. Unattributed English proverb, in Peter Linebaugh, *Stop, Thief! The Commons, Enclosure, and Resistance* (Oakland: PM Press, 2014), 1.

5. Jolanta Aidukaite, "Housing Policy Regime in Lithuania: Towards Liberalization and Marketization," *GeoJournal*, no. 79 (2014): 421–432.

6. Arūnas Juška, "Privatisation of State Security and Policing in Lithuania," in *Policing and Society*, no. 19 (2009): 226–246.

By 1988, the governing apparatus of Soviet Lithuania had already been sufficiently compromised to make way for the first known practices of squatting in the Užupis district of Vilnius—where artists seized buildings along the Neris River, converting them into communal studios. Indeed, amidst the crisis and then collapse of the socialist Eastern Bloc these new agential formations made their presence felt in both urban and rural territories. Drawing their agency from these divested zones, movements of commoning and enclosure asserted disparate claims over the use of resources and the former socialist infrastructures upon which they were cultivated. From anti-authoritarian squatting movements in East Berlin and Ljubljana,[7] to the new wave of enclosures and dispossessions carried out by former politicians-cum-business leaders, to everyday cultures of working-class pilfering and looting, antagonistic assertions over who had the rights to appropriation and access were practiced.

Such discrepancies made the need for the articulation of new juridical distinctions between just and unjust acts of appropriation urgent. As Peter Linebaugh deftly comments, the discourse of criminality "is capital's most ancient tool in the creation and control of the working class."[8] For it is through the scapegoat character of the criminal that the greater crimes of the ruling classes go undetected, enshrined as they are in the norms of law. With the state and financial mechanisms at their disposal, the emerging ruling classes in independent Lithuania assumed the role of these greater villains, rapidly appropriating large swaths of property. Lacking the policing and carceral apparatus that would otherwise serve to secure and legitimize their holdings, Lithuania's aspiring rulers came to depend on the informal, at times illicit, security services of the syndicates. The syndicates effectively took the role of a shadow state. Operating as unregistered private protection organizations, they deal with everything from: protection fees (10 percent

---

7. We find a clearly analogous demonstration of divested agency in East Berlin: "The squats in East Berlin at the beginning of the 1990s can only be viewed within the context of the explosive social changes that took place during the turnaround [*Wende*] and reunification. The political power vacuum of the Wende period, and the massive loss of authority on the part of the police and municipality, facilitated the large-scale occupation of vacant old buildings in the inner city. In addition, the GDR's housing policy, oriented towards new buildings, was creating the main basis of urban buildings for the squats. See Andrej Holm and Armin Kuhn, "Squatting and Urban Renewal," in *Squatting in Europe: Radical Spaces, Urban Struggles*, ed. Squatting Europe Kollective (Wivenhoe/New York/Port Watson: Minor Compositions, 2013), 169.

8. Linebaugh, *Stop, Thief!*, 43.

of earnings), extortion, property management, property distribution, smuggling and protection in logistics lines, enforcement of business contracts, to debt recovery.

While the criminal syndicates were able to partially secure the new enclosures of the ruling class, they did so at a risk of their legitimacy before the public. Enabled as they were through organized "criminal" groups, public suspicion grew around the rights of these agents to enclose and appropriate formally public resources (via the state).

Responding to the thefts of these greater villains, working-class commoning movements spread throughout the country. Like organized criminal groups, commoning formations embraced conditions of divestment as a basis for the articulation of social agency in urban and rural territories. By 1993, approximately 39.2 percent of the economy was rendered informal.[9] As one commenter bemoaned at the time, these everyday commoning practices came to be as much a threat to the formal economy and new state apparatus as the organized syndicates that operated under the purview of politicians and businessmen:

> While public fear has focused on the mafia and crimes of violence, more dangerous for the future fabric and morale of the Baltic States may be the almost universal habit of pilfering, fostered under Communism and entrenched by poverty. The practice is encouraged by the fact that even many educated people, let alone the masses, simply cannot understand why former criminals and criminal activities are now respectable, or the difference between making money from semilegal commercial activities and stealing outright from the office, shop or factory where you work.[10]

In rural territories, hit especially hard, open battles over the control of resources and land were inflamed. Of the state-owned and state-run *kolhoz* [collective farms] to which 450,000 families had belonged, privatization left a third of those families without legal vouchers, and therefore, without a possibility of privately appropriating publicly owned land and tools. Adding to this dispossession was a more general collapse of the social

9. Juška, "Privatisation of State Security and Policing in Lithuania."
10. Anatol Lieven, *The Baltic Revolution: Estonia, Latvia, Lithuania and the Path to Independence* (New Haven: Yale University Press, 1994).

infrastructures that surrounded these economic enterprises: administration, libraries, cultural houses, kindergartens, and medical aid outposts.[11]

And so the *Kolhozians* responded, assuming the standpoint of commoners, they usurped the new regime of private property and resisted the sale of themselves as labor power—showing particular interest in their former workplaces:

> Vast amounts of technological equipment, machinery and instruments in animal pens, and processing and storage facilities were either stolen or destroyed as their parts were dissembled and frequently sold for scrap metal. Bricks and roofs of *kolkhoz* facilities were stripped; and everything containing metal was taken away.[12]

The social infrastructure of the urban terrain would come to share the fate of its rural counterpart. Manufacturing steadily collapsed over the course of the preceding decades with output declining by more than one half between 1991–1993.[13] Like the kolkhoz, the factory was not only an economic unit but an integral component of a social infrastructure. The collapse of the factories marked the crisis of an entire mode of social, cultural, and political organization.

The fate of the Palace of Culture for Railway Workers is a telling instance of this crisis. Built in a typical Soviet Classicist style in 1956 and placed in the core of the emerging manufacturing zone that surrounded the railway district, the palace was full of cultural life and an integral institution for the new urban communities that arose alongside postwar industrial development. People would gather in the evenings for films and discos, come in the day to sit in the café and check out books from the library, or bring their children to the circus and other youth programs. In 1991, official activities ceased; the budget was withdrawn by the Ministry of Culture and Education. By 1993, an open call was published by the Ministry for a new director, ushering in a period of low-to-no-budget cultural entrepreneurship: "ten enthusiasts installed everything—toilets, the bar, the club

---

11. Arūnas Juška, "Rural Marginalization, Policing, and Crime in Lithuania," *Police Practice and Research*, no. 5 (2006): 431–447.

12. Juška, "Rural Marginalization," 438.

13. Arūnas Juška, "The Changing Character of Criminality and Policing in Post-Socialist Lithuania: From Fighting Organized Crime to Policing Marginal Populations?" *Crime, Law & Social Change*, no. 41 (2004): 161–177.

hall—with their own hands in three months."[14] Although the cultural operations of the building recommenced, neighbors found the "independent" programing far less accessible than in the previously budgeted programs of the socialist era.[15] Precariously organized as a semicommercial entity, consistently divested by the Ministry, the building would be abandoned by 1998 as the ruble crisis ripped through the region. Taking advantage of this moment, the building was squatted. The squatters cultivated a social common with living quarters, a kitchen, an infoshop, and a venue, inspiring the spread of like-minded autonomous clubs and social centers in a handful of cities across the country.[16]

Commoning as and beyond Survival

Communal land grabs, everyday pilfering of workplaces, and the looting of newly enclosed infrastructures made evident a desire to collectively appropriate and control the shared concerns of everyday life. Much more than a spontaneous reaction to hard times, these commoning practices in Lithuania were informed by a communally constituted working-class knowledge carefully cultivated over many years. *Blatas,* the self-organized practice of the appropriation and resale of resources from the assigned workplace (abundant both in the rural *kolhozes* and the urban factories), combined with other semi-autonomous communal reproduction practices—e.g., trading produce from state assigned urban gardens plots or subsidizing holidays through small scale import businesses—equipping divested agents with a skill set for the articulation of semi-autonomous assertions over social space.[17]

Such agential formations developed in the semantic slippages over the status of property and the rights of its appropriation under state socialism. As one researcher reflecting on the social conditions that gave way to blatas

---

14. Domininkas Kunčinas, "Kablys: Alternative Culture by Hook or by Crook," *Lithuanian Music Link*, 2008, https://www.mic.lt/en/discourses/lithuanian-music-link/no22-january-december-2019/domininkas-kuncinas-kablys-alternative-culture-hook-or-crook/.

15. Tadas Šarūnas, "The Pleasures and Pains of a Changing City," presentation facilitated by Naujininkai Commons, Luna6, Vilnius, November 10, 2021.

16. Kunčinas, "Kablys."

17. While these practices could be called "survival responses" to tough times, survivalism risks reducing the knowledges and skills informing such practices to a sub-social biological response. Such a reduction is especially problematic in the East where we face a neocolonial knowledge regime that has a way of erasing our social power and the histories of its organization in leftist formations.

accounts, "State property was declared to be a public good and supposed to be guarded by everyone . . . but 'public' could also be interpreted as quasi-private, which was grasped in the everyday sayings: 'public' means that part of it is mine."[18] Similarly, women in our district, Naujininkai, decided that a part of state land adjacent to their new housing blocks was "theirs" to guard and till, and then went on to further invite their friends and neighbors to join them.

FIGURE 5.1. *Naujininkai community gardens in Spring 2021. Photo by Vaiva Aglinskas.*

Between 1969 and 1972, five- and nine-story apartment blocks were constructed on top of the hill, and probably some of the first residents already started to use the adjacent slope for gardening plots, which are said to have been handed down over generations. Prior to the mass housing constructions, this site was probably a homestead with a well and orchard. Many of the fruit trees remain, as does the well, although the poor quality of the water renders it unusable. Along the slope, about a dozen garden plots were made, some are fenced in (even with barbed wire and locks), some have makeshift greenhouse structures, while other patches of strawberries remain barely noticeable in the taller surrounding grasses. Today, a handful of older women continue to cultivate their garden plots and do not shy

---

18. Alena Ledeneva, "Between Gift and Commodity: The Phenomenon of Blat," *Cambridge Journal of Anthropology* 19, no. 3 (1996): 47.

away from also setting up shop on the sidewalk along the outer wall of the supermarket Maxima around the corner to informally sell them. Neither a reflection of the profit logic of the formal economy nor a mere question of social dignity, these gardens are expressive of a regional form of social reproduction that points towards a commonist worldview. As Ledeneva comments:

> By pooling resources, by engaging in informal practices, by self-provisioning, and by the skillful use of social networks and families, it can be argued, people avoided entrapment in the Soviet regime. They became actors who engaged in relations with others to get what they can out of the existing system. To conclude, *blat* cannot be adequately grasped in terms of informal economic practices [. . .]. It implies ties of reciprocity within personal networks, rather than profit-oriented activities and market-type exchanges, on which informal economic practices are often based.[19]

Stavros Stavrides addresses how such "survival responses" are more than just adaptive practices devoid of political standpoints, considering the cultures of solidarity they hold together as pivotal to revolutionary social movements, "solidarity then a crucial element of a future emancipated society, is not discovered ideologically, as an alternative value, but is distilled from the everyday experiences of small and large urban communities. Obviously, not only solidarity grows in these everyday struggles for survival. It is, however, a movement, deeply rooted in these communities, that can fertilize solidarity actions against any prevailing and often hopeless atomism."[20] Such a society in movement could be said to take root in the dynamic between these everyday practices of blatas, communal cultures of reproduction, and the spread of anti-authoritarian clubs and infoshops, inspired by the example of the former Palace of Culture for Railway Workers. It could just as well be said to take place in the dynamics between the wave of strikes in the late socialist era and the coordination of neighborhood kitchens that enabled extended withdrawals from waged work. Rather than an elevation

---

19. Alena Ledeneva, *Russia's Economy of Favors: Blat, Networking and Informal Exchange* (Cambridge: Cambridge University Press, 1998), 51.
20. Stavros Stavrides, *Common Space: The City as Commons* (London: Zed Books, 2018).

of survival practices to the level of consciousness, the autonomist club movement and strike waves grew in dynamic relations of reciprocity and cohabitation.

Just as Marx arrived at the idea of communism in seeing the Prussian peasants' theft of wood from the forest as a universal declaration against the rights of private appropriation, regional practices of blatas and communal subsistence may be embraced as components of a commonist infrastructure. Rather than simply sub-social, spontaneously organized tendencies, we could see these movements as involved in "worlding": articulating forms of organization that are more than fragmentary responses to the general decomposition of life under capitalism.

Regeneration and its Discontents

> A theory of gentrification will need to explain the historical process of capital devalorization in the inner city and the precise way in which this devalorization produces the possibility of profitable reinvestment.
> —Neil Smith, *The New Urban Frontier*

> The control of space was no longer just about the control of objects in space; space itself produced and was now bought and sold as an 'ultimate object of exchange.'
> —Henri Lefebvre, *The Urban Revolution*

The ruble crisis in 1998 changed the course of commoning struggles, subsuming the divested agencies that engendered them, and the illicit criminal economies to which they were adjacent. As trade with Russia froze, the Lithuanian economy and state quickly reoriented to the West—by 2000, the EU had become Lithuania's primary export market.[21] Between 1996 and 2000, Western foreign investment grew at astonishing rates: from 390 million to 2.2 billion euros.[22] Chasing quick returns, Western banks revitalized the economy through the cheap—but volatile—consumer loans market, rather than the slower but more secure manufacturing and infrastructural sectors.[23]

Arriving with this new flow of capital came a large-scale urban development vision targeting the city's future commercial cores, the Old Town,

---

21. Juška, "Privatisation of State Security and Policing in Lithuania."
22. Juška, "The Changing Character of Criminality and Policing in Post-Socialist Lithuania."
23. Juška, "The Changing Character of Criminality and Policing in Post-Socialist Lithuania."

Užupis, and the financial district Šnipiškės. Divested already by Soviet-era urban planning, which directed capital into the building of mass modern housing complexes or "sleeping districts" around the peripheries of cities, the undermaintained core was rendered less than attractive to the weak, still emerging, private real estate market. Indeed, walking through the central streets of Vilnius in 1996, one could encounter hundreds of idle, undermaintained municipal properties. Although the municipality had already begun its revitalization efforts a few years back, taking out loans from local banks for the refurbishment and then private sale of these properties, the scale and pace of such processes would radically increase in 1998, when the city was granted a development loan from the Western International Bank for Reconstruction and Development.[24]

The radical devalorization of urban space and social infrastructure in the former eras of Soviet inner-city divestment and neoliberal collapse fertilized the soils for an advantageous period of financialized "revitalization" over the next decade—but not without resistance and discontent.

Securitization of Capital

The commonized spaces and illicit economies cultivated over the collapse era came to present a significant barrier to Western capital. The unruly agencies engendered under conditions of divestment threatened the security, and hence prospects, of foreign direct investment. Early dialogues with the EU began over security matters. Divested agency was to be repressed, subsumed, and mutated in the approaching era of financialized revitalization. Organized crime syndicates, for instance, were in part repressed—via militarized, state-of-exception style crack downs—while on the other hand, incorporated into the formal economy and state as registered "security firms." The largest global security company, Falck Security Group, effectively took control over 40 percent of services, which it still occupies.[25] Such a resecuritization of social space thus not only ensured the security of foreign private investment but also allowed for the rebuilding of the state apparatus, which regained an essential power—the taxation of economic affairs. Yet, with all the capital pouring in, public infrastructure and welfare

24. Harald Standl and Dovilė Krupickaitė, "Gentrification in Vilnius (Lithuania): The example of Užupis," *Europa Regional* 12, no. 1 (2004): 42–51.
25. Juška, "Privatisation of State Security and Policing in Lithuania," 240.

services continued to be dismantled. As one city planning official grimly observed in 2000:

> What kind of housing policy can be implemented and by whom? The state and local governments are practically withdrawn from this sector. Housing has been left as a problem of private developers or the population. This means that cities and municipalities only carry the function of planning and private investors build houses. Renovation is carried out at the expenses of the house owners. Can we call it housing policy? Is there any policy? There is no policy.[26]

That same year, the first gated community appeared in Lithuania—exemplifying a model of governance that would promise security, well-being, and "community" only for those who could afford it.[27] By 1998, the wealthiest 10 percent held eight times more purchasing power than the poorest decile (25.31 percent and 3.17 percent).[28] In subordinating the semi-autonomous territories through which social reproduction had been articulated to the path of financialized revitalization, the new "social" security of capital was mirrored in a growing social insecurity of everyday life.

The fate of the Naujininkai gardens is telling here. In 2006 the destruction of the valley adjacent to the gardens began, to make way for the largest infrastructural project to date in independent Lithuania, subsidized by the EU. This new logistics route for trade meant the uprooting of the orchard, greenery, and the demolition of twenty-five dwelling spaces—with over 500 properties forcibly bought from local residents to make way for the highway.[29]

---

26. See Jolanta Aidukaite, "Housing Policy Regime in Lithuania: Towards Liberalization and Marketization," *GeoJournal* 79, no. 4 (2014): 421–432.

27. As noted by Anastasia Sosunova, "The first such neighborhood in Lithuania, Bendorėliai, was constructed in 2001, in Avižieniai, a suburb of Vilnius. It was founded by a person who returned from the USA and decided to try and apply the model of American suburban neighborhoods in Lithuania. The idea of fenced off and guarded neighborhoods was a new thing in the country's real estate market at the time." See Anastasia Sosunova, *Express Method*, ed. Vaida Sepanovaitė (Vilnius: Swallow Gallery, 2021).

28. Juška, "The Changing Character of Criminality and Policing in Post-Socialist Lithuania."

29. DELFI, "Vilniaus aplinkkelio kaina—po 50 tūkst. litų už arą," *Delfi*, March 17, 2008, https://www.delfi.lt/verslas/nekilnojamas-turtas/vilniaus-aplinkkeliu-kaina-po-50-tukst-lt-uz-ara.d?id=16356007.

Locals expressed concerns during the construction, ranging from uncertainties about whether an off-ramp for an exit into the district will be built; children having to walk through a dark path in the woods to get to school; no sidewalks or walkways to navigate the muddy construction sites; and the poor quality of the triple-pane windows promised to the nearest residents to block out sound. Many were unsatisfied with the compensation they received in battles over the sale of their housing, cottages, and land in the way of eminent domain. Residents surrounding the gardens expressed deep disappointment about the road—polluting their gardens and communities, subordinating the needs of social connectivity to the needs of capital's circulation—with whooshing cars and exhaust fumes taking the place of the orchard and greenery.

Meanwhile the collective squatting the Railroad Workers Palace, having struggled to maintain the large and consistently divested infrastructure, confronted a critical threshold in its degradation by 2002 when a second electrical fire led to the commoners' displacement. The building was eventually sold off and converted into a successful commercial, underground-style techno club. The former commoners eventually returned in 2005 after discovering a large basement under the building, and ever since have been left at the mercy of a rental agreement with the site's new private landlord.

Throughout the former socialist East, divested agents resisted this new cycle of neoliberal urban development. Commoning, squatting, and communal reproduction practices swept through our region.[30] The social claims made over the city of Vilnius by commoning and worlding movements came to an iconic turning point in 2005, when a municipally owned cinema was occupied in protest of its sale to developers.

Built in 1965, by the early 1990s much of its ownership had fallen into the hands of the Vilnius municipality. Despite being recently renovated and actively running, in 2002 it was auctioned off by the municipal bureau to a private real estate company with plans to reorganize land use from "cinema" into an apartment complex (albeit retaining a small cinema with several small halls that seemed hardly convincing). Only

---

30. A very important reference point for us comes from the research of comrades in the Balkans, who connect such commoning movements in their recent book. See Iva Čukić and Jovana Timotijević, eds., *Spaces of Commoning: Urban Commons in the Ex-YU Region* (Belgrade: Ministry of Space/Institute for Urban Politics, 2020).

three years after the renovation, the cinema announced its closure; an announcement that instigated one of the most analyzed acts of organized protest in recent decades.[31]

The occupation that followed not only defended the site as a publicly owned infrastructure but through the social transformations of roles that took place, made a claim to its common social use. Composed of anarchists, artists, and the broader public, the commoners engaged in a wide array of practices. Hosted under the banner of a "protest-lab," activities ranged from communal meals to concerts to screenings and architectural interventions.[32] Although initially framed as an issue of the municipal handling of cultural spaces—indeed, in this period, the Vilnius municipality allowed several other significant properties for culture to crumble through divestment— the discussion extended into a discontent with the dubious legality of the municipality's dealings with private developers and the planning of public space in general. The occupiers delved into documents showing how the municipality had strategically devalued the property before selling it, in addition to changing its zoning from public to private use to facilitate the private interests of developers.

The occupation marked a shifting point in public consciousness about the municipality's responsibility for guarding and maintaining public infrastructure while also demonstrating the power of commoning movements in the shaping of urban space for years to come.[33] Yet, while this commoning movement marked a significant victory over the real estate company and the general movement of enclosure of social space in the city (the municipality retracted its sale), the cinema, left idle and out of the public eye for some years to come, was eventually sold to an art-collecting business couple who demolished it to make way for a museum. Having amassed a significant collection of Lithuanian art, this duo would by 2018 open a privately

31. Nell Harrison, "The end of Lietuva cinema, the death of community culture," *Baltic Times*, August 6, 2005, https://www.baltictimes.com/news/articles/12887; Geert Lovink, "Interview with Nomeda & Gediminas. Hacking Public Spaces in Vilnius: Politics of a new media space inside the Lietuva (soviet) cinema" (June 20, 2005), posted by Stevphen, *Interactivist Info Exchange*, July 15, 2005, http://dev.autonomedia.org/node/4527?fbclid =IwAR13e8YuGKRxsfR0mpiX1dKOh_Y-YvU-UcRS4JgHDjnNZ_jDBybk5DhnyAQ.

32. For a good timeline of the "Pro-testo laboratorija" project, see http://www.vilma.cc/ LIETUVA/en_index.php?l=LT&mid=0&nid=0.

33. See Lina Michelkevice, "Between Art and Politics: Pro-test Laboratory as Establishment of Public Space," *Goethe-Institut Litauen* (2013), https://www.goethe.de/ins/lt/lt/kul/ mag/20550207.html); Skaidra Trilupaitytė, "Artistic Protest and (Political) Critique: Vilnius Examples of the First Decade of the XXI Century," *Art History & Criticism* 11 (2015): 5–21.

owned, yet publicly cofinanced museum in Vilnius, the MO Modern Art Museum, built by Daniel Libeskind. Taking as a trophy the former sign of the cinema and placing it in its sculpture park, the museum stands as an iconic symbol of capital's triumph over the commons in Vilnius while also demonstrating how the municipality—faced with the threat of the building's appropriation by commoners—partially conceded to its protection for social use. The building, after all, is not (yet) a parking garage or condo complex, but a museum.[34]

The Regenerate City

> Community is killed off only to be 'regenerated' in zombie-like form, a living dead state of social (non)reproduction and officially orchestrated sham spectacles of being together.
> —Anthony Iles and Josephine Berry Slater, *No Room to Move*

The 2008 global crisis hit the Baltics hard. Severe job losses and a sovereign debt crisis made way for a deeper immiseration of everyday life, prompting the first open riot in the independent republic of Lithuania's history. Responding to this new reality and inspired by the international movements of the squares, Occupy Riga emerged in neighboring Latvia in 2011. Occupy Riga critically called attention to the idle properties lining the city's streets, gesturing at their occupation by slapping "Free Riga" stickers onto them. While Occupy Riga phased out alongside the international revolts it was inspired by, Free Riga continues. Recuperating the spirit of Occupy, the group transformed into a grassroots real-estate entity. It has gone on to successfully broker deals with private landlords and the municipality for temporary rent-free/reduced leasing of idle properties to independent cultural formations, in return for investments in their upkeep carried out by the artist members of the initiatives and the cultural enterprises operating

---

34. The same public-private partnership goes for the other major art institution to pop up in the past decade, Rupert. Owned by another wealthy business family, the building was almost completely financed by the EU on the family's private land, which was zoned by the city as a park. While the EU Development Funds stipulated its mixed commercial use as a start-up incubator and residency for fifteen years before it can be sold on the private market, the owners indeed were thinking ahead, violating EU agreements by laying out plumbing for kitchens in the units. Although the construction of the kitchens was frozen by EU regulators and flagged as a violation, the plumbing remains all set up; the units are only waiting to be sold off as condos on the most expensive land in all of Lithuania.

in their complexes or buildings, including a hostel, bars, art galleries, housing, and concert venues.

An analogous phenomenon had already appeared in Vilnius in 2010, when the newly elected liberal mayor Artūras Zuokas opened the doors of a sizeable and centrally located former Ministry of Health building to artistic communities, free of charge, for a *strategically* ambiguous duration of time. It is notable that the self-organized repurposing of this formally public institution as studios, exhibition space, concert hall, screening venue, etc.—now called Fluxus Ministry—in many ways took the same forms as the commoning struggle that captured the public's support a few years back in the Lietuva Cinema occupation.

Indeed, Fluxus Ministry and Free Riga strategically utilize divested agency, inviting autonomous assertions over undermaintained and abandoned urban spaces that *resemble* the same commoning and worlding processes otherwise repressed by the state and suffocated by the real estate market. Yet, a fundamental difference between these entities and commoning formations appears behind the scenes. In only a year's time, Zuokas announced the Fluxus Ministry would be closed, the building having been sold to a private developer. It was rapidly repurposed as start-up offices and a coffee chain. The cultural community, thrown out on the streets, surrendered without any organized acts of rebellion beyond a few angry articles in the press.[35] Meanwhile, Free Riga situates itself as a real estate developer, openly collaborating in municipal level development schemes: bargaining off the maintenance labor and value-adding creative charm of cultural communities for compromised, short-term agencies over urban space.

Clearly, capital's domination isn't only based on the power of control (say in the relation between boss and employee or cop and civilian) but extraction, i.e., capital can very well allow and even facilitate activities based upon commonist relationalities (sharing, commoning, and social use over profit), insofar as it retains the capacity for their eventual containment and extraction as sources of profit.[36]

As public resources are sold off, social amenities are continuously withdrawn and public infrastructures undermined, the "activation" of

---

35. Agnese Čivle, "The Messenger of Fluxus For the 21st Century," *Arterritory*, December 23, 2014, https://arterritory.com/en/visual_arts/interviews/12301-the_messenger_of_fluxus_for_the_21st_century/.

36. For an expanded commentary on why sharing and other noncapitalist relationalities are not equitable with communism, see Leon de Mattis, "Reflections on the Call," in *Communization and its Discontents: Contestation, Critique, and Contemporary Struggle*, ed. Benjamin Noys (Wivenhoe/New York/Port Watson: Minor Compositions, 2012), 61–84.

self-organizing communities appears as a means for reducing the costs of social reproduction to appropriate greater profits. These strategies are connected with a transnational development policy called "creative regeneration."[37] Regeneration policies have since appeared in Vilnius as a widespread tactic for revalorizing the idle and abandoned urban infrastructures of socialism's past. Cynically handing divested buildings and infrastructures to communities who temporarily dress them up as a social commons, the municipality turns around to displace them moments later, when investors are ready to enclose these now enchanted assets as commodities for the market.

Capital's Social Fix

> One never maps a territory that one doesn't contemplate appropriating.
> —The Invisible Committee, *The Coming Insurrection*

The fact that people were using state-owned land to grow vegetables at the very outer edge of the city had been ignored by the municipality for decades until just recently, when the entire district became a prioritized area for regeneration (of housing, infrastructure, etc.) under "Vilnius Connect." When plans to develop the territory around the Naujininkai common garden into a public space—that would include the gardens— were introduced to the community in 2019, many of the commoners reacted apologetically and defensively since they understood they were using state land. Many were surprised that they were going to be allowed to continue gardening, and that they were even encouraged to do so. In the future, the land will remain state-owned, but will be leased by the Vilnius City Municipality, which will then sublease it to the gardeners for a yet to be decided symbolic fee.

Drafting of the law for urban gardening began in 2018 and it seems to have been officially passed in 2021.[38] Whatever the conditions wind up being for this garden, the effect will undoubtedly be a formalization and institutionalization of a spatial practice/use that people had

---

37. For a thorough history of the origins of regeneration in the UK, see Anthony Iles and Josephine Berry Slater, *No Room to Move: Radical Art and the Regenerate City* (London: Mute Books, 2010).

38. The law developed out of an URBACT project that was begun in 2018, which developed guidelines/a rubric for how urban gardening might take space in the city according to five-year contracts.

established far more autonomously. While the legal paperwork may offer a sense of stability or rigidity, the developer's vision for this space will further "expose" the gardens, highlighting them as a focal point for panoramic lookouts and benches lining a new walkway along the rim of the slope.[39]

The municipality's inclusion of the gardens in its district regeneration program typifies a broader shift in governance—a move from the ad hoc approaches of creative revitalization of the previous era to their generalization in the present as a systemic urban development strategy. The refractory, antagonistic, social claims to urban space made by yesterday's divested agents has today been systematically incorporated into governance strategies as a "social fix" for the reproductive crisis engendered by capital's ruthless drive for profit: outsourcing the costs of asset maintenance and social reproduction onto communities, temporarily displacing the social antagonisms that come with the general onslaught of for-profit development futures.

As affordable housing exponentially diminishes,[40] the municipality has doubled its efforts in the last few years to sell off properties and key infrastructures (for example, state electricity provision has been completely privatized between 2020–2022). An "active-through-use" model has been employed to incentivize social/cultural organizations to repair the state's divested, idle, undermaintained units as well as to offer social services free of charge for at-risk populations; in exchange for lease agreements—from five to twenty years—set below market rates. The precarious status of these agreements with the municipality was made clear in 2021 in a grim turn of events on the terms of rental. The municipality removed the clause in the lease which stated that the venue can be rented until sold at public auction and that the municipality can one-sidedly and without a reason break the contract with only six months notice.[41]

---

39. You can already find renderings of the future gardens on the profiles of adjacent properties on real estate websites.

40. Vilnius has recently been seeing a construction boom not only in office spaces but also in residential real estate. The average price of such newly constructed housing in 2020 ran at around 2030 euro per square meter, while people's average net wage was 950 euro. 6,000 apartments were sold in Vilnius in 2019, leaving a reserve of 5,500 apartments waiting to be bought. Meanwhile 1,646 people are waiting in line to rent social housing from the state.

41. This change in agreement was announced here, https://vilnius.lt/lt/finansai-ir-turtas/vilniaus-miesto-savivaldybes-administracija-nuomoja-nekilnojamaji-turta-skroblu-g-27-vilniu-je-vieso-konkurso-budu-pagal-iveiklinimo-ideja-2/.

Nonprofit organizations run by underpaid or volunteer-based subjects are expected to pick up the slack of public services as the economy is increasingly restructured along neoliberal lines. Included in regeneration yet excluded from real stakes in the power to decide on a district's future, such schemes operate through what Anthony Iles and Josephine Berry Slater—via Giorgio Agamben—have called "inclusive exclusions":

> [T]he idea that 'inclusion' into collective articulations of desire, or forms of group self-expression, can solve or significantly ameliorate the structural nature of social inequality is at best idealistic. . . . Such is the rhetorical trap of 'openness'—a mediating operation by which intensities and antagonisms are diffused. How then can 'communities' manifest without lending themselves to the state's need to 'activate' them for a pre-defined purpose (social reproduction as labour power), becomes an increasingly fraught issue.[42]

While our "inclusion" may be compromised and fraught, in being subsumed we gain a certain leverage within urban development processes, the success and failure of which now partially depend on our active participation within them. In leasing out their properties to social and cultural initiatives instead of simply selling them off to real estate developers (which they are currently doing in great numbers), they have inadvertently supported the growth of a common urban infrastructure for the city. We ask ourselves: what would it mean to defend these sites from private appropriation in the future? And to what extent could the commons be cultivated as a unified standpoint—and thus strategy— among the range of organizations currently occupying these sites?

Beyond the City of Enclaves

Returning to our starting point—the Naujininkai district—we conclude by taking a first step towards the commonist horizon through a mapping of possible solidarities between commonist formations organized by divested agents in municipal properties around our district—two out of the three of them operating under the active-through-use regeneration policy. Beginning by profiling each formation—its agreement with the municipality, history

---

42. Iles and Berry Slater, *No Room to Move*, 34.

of divestment, current commoning (or aspiring) practice, and threats of enclosure—we address here what Stavros Stavrides refers to as "thresholds," and how to cultivate these between the profiled "enclaves" to both achieve the immediate need of unenclosing one (the migrant detention center) and for the long-term goal of building a culture and economy of solidarity between the many other groups, spaces, and organizations in and beyond the city. It is only from the practical building of solidarity through thresholds that our shared political principles may be cultivated for a movement against the "development" looming in our respective futures.

FIGURE 5.2. *Collected aid items in the migrant detention center in Naujininkai, Fall 2021.*

Enclave no. 1: Migrant Detention Center

Down the street from Luna6 is the newly formed detention center for migrants who have crossed the border from Belarus to seek refuge in the EU. The walled-off territory includes two large buildings—a four-story school and a four-story dorm with grated windows. The two yards are connected by a narrow footpath hemmed in by the wall that separates this territory from the adjacent parking lot of the Orthodox church of Aleksandr

Nevski.[43] Built in 1960, the school and dorm complex functioned as a juvenile detention center for girls [*mergaiciu kolonija*]. In 1964, the school was turned into a professional-technical school for children from orphanages, which also provided the girls in the detention center with primary and secondary education, supplemented with many extracurricular activities and three apprenticeship training workshops.

After 1991, the correctional facility continued to function in the four-story brick building as the "Vilnius Children's Socialization Center."[44] This was liquidated in 2018 as part of a joint Lithuanian government and EU structural funds project aimed at modernizing and consolidating socialization centers in rural locations.[45] The decision to shut down the centers in Vilnius and Kaunas (the two largest cities in Lithuania) and relocate their residents to peripheral locations where they would be "surrounded by nature" was seen as a mistake by many employees who raised legitimate concerns about whether removal from an urban milieu that provides both cultural stimulation and a wide range of qualified specialists would contribute towards "socialization." Some intuited that the decision was made to pave the way for business interests to claim central urban real estate. Indeed, shortly after, the detention center building was transferred to *Turto Bankas* [Centralized Public Property Management] to be auctioned off, but in the summer of 2019, the building's status changed again and was handed over to the Vilnius municipality to house the homeless while the original shelter in Naujoji Vilnia—a district situated far from the city center—underwent renovations. As promised, the shelter was "temporary," and in September 2021 the night shelter returned to the now renovated building in in Naujoji Vilnia. That very same week, the process began to convert the building in Naujininkai into a shelter to house migrants and refugees who

---

43. This church was built in 1896–1898, together with a school building which functioned until 1915. From 1937 to 1960, the Orthodox sisters of the Order of Mary Magdalene oversaw this complex and rebuilt the church themselves after a 1944 air raid. Under the Soviet regime, the church was nationalized, and in 1960, the twenty-eight nuns were displaced to other convents and the territory was turned into a juvenile correctional facility for girls, which is when the four-story dorm was built. After Independence, the church was renewed and returned to believers in 1990, although it stood idle until its renovation in 2012, and in 2015 the sisters of the Order of Mary Magdalene reoccupied the premises.

44. The girls who lived in the dorm attended the adjacent school together with students from the "*vaiku globos namai.*" In 2016 the NGO *Atsigrezk i Vaikus* [Return to the Children] installed a playground and painted the inner walls of the courtyard. In 2009, around fifty girls were living there (only thirteen in the summer months) and by 2018, when this institution was terminated, only nine girls lived there (serviced by fifty employees).

45. The project was called "Infrastructural Modernization of Children's Socialization Centers" (2014–2020).

had arrived in Lithuania via Belarus over the summer and required better conditions than camps could offer once the cold season started.

The fact that this space has been turned into a space of care (albeit carceral) offers a standpoint for its repurposing as a commons. The school building, for instance, left idle after the closure of the girls' socialization center, has now been converted into a space for youth education, sports, and dwelling. And while the complex is a "refuge" for an international community of Kurdish, Iraqi, and Afghani migrant asylum seekers, it is also a space of punishment, stigmatization, enclosure, and surveillance. The making of this space of enclosure into a commons requires a movement of *unenclosure*, or as the CareNotes Collective would call it, *deinstitutionalization*.[46] The reclaiming of this migrant prison as a transnational space of hospitality and commoning has already begun through community-led efforts to build thresholds, such as: clothing and food drives as well as protests organized through district networks surrounding Luna6. Ultimately, the goal of such social solidarity and community support would be to make refugee camps obsolete.

At the moment, two large-scale housing/retail developments have already claimed the territories of a former glass factory and a professional driving school[47] that bracket the part of Naujininkai closest to the changes promised by Vilnius Connect. The detention center, already put on auction years ago, risks being sold off and repurposed by developers—perhaps as a "tech park" for young professionals, as happened with Sapiegos Park in Antakalnis. The risk of enclosure is therefore not only a threat of the complex's continued use as a carceral facility but also in its possible future commercialization and "regeneration" as a resource only accessible to those of a certain social class. Notably, such commercialized enclosure has already taken this path at another former prison in the city center which was converted into a creative hub, bar, and concert venue via the "active-through-use" policy.

Finally, a threat of continued enclosure and displacement comes from some of the residents of Naujininkai, especially those living adjacent to the walled-in territory who have interpreted the series of state-initiated transformations of the building's function as an act of deliberate divestment.

---

46. CareNotes Collective, *For Health Autonomy: Horizons of Care Beyond Austerity—Reflections from Greece* (Brooklyn: Common Notions, 2020).

47. This facility was auctioned off in June 2021 and plays into the broader trend of ridding Vilnius of garages. It also shows clear prioritization of real estate profit and prestige over workers' professionalization.

In this case, it is not the emptiness of an idle space, but rather the use and inhabitation of the building by various vulnerable groups that raises concerns about fiscal as well as socio-symbolic devaluation of the neighborhood. Such concerns were loudly voiced at the community meeting announcing the arrival of the migrant detention center. In Naujininkai, housing of the most vulnerable has become a point of contention because some residents feel resentful about the state offering care and accommodation to certain groups while failing to acknowledge and provide for their needs. "We need a psychiatric facility in this district, not a refugee center," fumed one resident over the homeless shelter's conversion into a migrant detention center.

Enclave no. 2: Vilnius Social Club

The Vilnius Social Club has been active in our district for many years as a street-based youth workers' initiative. In 2019, after a quick but thorough renovation of a municipally owned storefront which had been completely abandoned, Vilnius Social Club settled into their new "home." As they say in their report, they "rented premises from the Vilnius City Municipality on preferential terms at Dzūkų str. 37 until 2028. The renovation of the premises will cost approximately 80,000 euro," from which the majority came from sponsors and the rest from in-kind support: carpentry services, donations of kitchen utensils, furniture, etc.

Vilnius Municipality sees itself as a "partner" of this social organization, as one can read in its announcement concerning the establishment of the Vilnius Social Club premises. This is also how it is communicated in the media by head of Vilnius Municipality Administration, who calls for more social organizations to receive such "help" under the active-through-use strategy.[48] The reports show that this municipal help funds between 14 to 25 percent of the Club's annual budget, with the Lithuanian state additionally contributing about a third.

Vilnius Social Club is a progressive secular organization and understands its job as providing guidance and tools for local youth to self-organize rather than performing a disciplinary or moral role. For instance, the kitchen was placed in the front of the space to serve as a drop-in center

---

48. For program details, see https://m.diena.lt/naujienos/vilnius/miesto-pulsas/
sostines-savivaldybe-keturias-patalpas-atiduos-vilnieciu-idejoms-igyvendinti-1006755.

offering food twice a week. Unlike typical welfare organizations, the club actively resists assuming the position of a hierarchical and punitive service provider: they give youth autonomy over what they eat and guide them, when desired, in food preparation. When youth groups drop in, they are given a credit card to independently make purchases and then cook communally in the space. Every month the club also prepares food packages for district families, organized by the youth themselves.

Vilnius Social Club is building *thresholds* between its function as a district-based hub for youth groups and their families, through its activities, twice a week, with international youth at the migrant detention center down the street. It has also begun collaborations with Luna6, whose community has joined them in these activities, amongst other migrant solidarity initiatives.

The area immediately surrounding the club has seen a new condo complex built in the last two years—a divested wooden municipal house demolished to make way for it—with another neighboring abandoned shopfront slated for demolition and condo construction. While the "at-risk" youth service may be essential for developers and the municipality in smoothing out conflicts between the area's new "invested" residents and the divested, impoverished, ethnically oppressed minorities of its "past," it's not hard to imagine a change of heart after the area's "successful" development—resulting in the replacement of this social service with a chic café, for instance.

Enclave no. 3: SODAS 2123

In 2019, the SODAS 2123 cultural center, operated and curated by the Lithuanian Interdisciplinary Artists' Association (LIAA), started settling into a complex of buildings walking distance from both the Station district and Naujininkai. One building was erected right after the Second World War; another group of buildings were added in 1974. Until 2005–2007, it operated as a boarding school for children with special needs, when the school was joined with a similar facility in an outer suburb of Vilnius. Until 2015, an Adult Learning Center offered various classes, from sewing courses to Spanish lessons. It was eventually abandoned by the municipality, becoming a hideout for youngsters and other visitors, some of them previously schooled there and who still come here now.

In 2019, the operators of SODAS 2123, the Lithuanian Interdisciplinary Artists' Association (LIAA), together with other individuals from the cultural field, successfully answered an open call for use of the site issued by the Vilnius City Municipality (the first of many). In 2019, the LIAA signed a twenty-year lease and started the renovations as required by it—some with the help of the municipality itself, but mostly through self-financing, volunteer labor of the new artist tenants, and bartering. Public cultural activities, such as visual arts exhibitions and performances, began taking place in 2020.

As of 2022, SODAS 2123 is the biggest cultural complex in Lithuania, having a large amount of space and involving around sixty tenant contracts that cover approximately 150 people in individual or shared artist studios, cultural organizations' offices (e.g., Architektūros Fondas and Design Foundation, publisher Hubris, animation production studios, etc.), and public cultural venues. The latter are and have been galleries or project spaces, such as: Swallow, co-run by an NC member; Trivium; Atletika (run by LIAA); and various student-run spaces. There is also a community-based café and concert space, the Empty Brain Resort. There are workshops for graphic design and printing, analog cinema and photography, production skills (crafting, building, and cutting from wood and metal), artistic-scientific research, also people working with sound, and with light installations. On the upper floor of one building is an artist residency with private living and shared communal spaces. In the cellar, one can find studios decked out for rehearsal, and in the adjacent complex, there is a large hall for events. There is also an urban garden which operates depending on the season and the availability of the people involved.

Such a variety of residents and their activities comes out of the idea for SODAS 2123 to run on, as LIAA say, an "exchange economy," in which the residents complement each other and barter skills and goods. While there is an emphasis on the inner ecosystem, SODAS 2123 is open—and is also contractually obligated by the landlord municipality to be open—to various publics. SODAS 2123 residents put on public events, such as screenings, gallery openings, community markets, performances, etc., which take place weekly and are mostly free of charge. Concerts are put on by the residents or by the LIAA. Another side of accessibility is with even more specific publics in mind, such as those who come for goods and services offered by tenants as their mode of operation and sustenance, or just by individual resident artists connecting with their own communities.

In February 2022, the SODAS 2123 enclave showed its capacity to cultivate thresholds—alongside other cultural organizations in Lithuania—by offering their space and support for those seeking shelter after fleeing war in Ukraine. Artist residency facilities were opened as living spaces, along with individual residents who wanted to offer their own studios. This threshold may very well welcome the emergence of new thresholds in the future, such as developing relations with the migrant detention center in Naujininkai. While SODAS 2123 has a mission of creating space for those working in culture in a broad sense, as well as conditions for showing their creative work in an accessible way, there is a great abundance of operators in one place with sets of skills that could be put to good use creating strong ties with the neighboring communities as well as those in urgent need. In a spirit of a threshold, these skills could also be offered for maintenance of the Vilnius Social Club building and cofacilitating its social and educational activities for children and young people.

Cultivating stronger and wider thresholds, such as by extending SODAS 2123's "exchange economy" into a solidarity economy, might be the best shot at surviving what is coming after the contract ends—possible, if not assured, displacement.

The lease signed by the LIAA and the Vilnius municipality is for twenty years but having observed such infamous examples in Vilnius as Fluxus Ministry, the group's trust in this contract is low. There are few in the building who think these municipal rentals for cultural organizations is anything other than "business as usual" for getting artists to refurbish idle venues—divested by the municipality itself—in prime locations so it may later sell to private investors. Therefore, the renters are reluctant to create long-term attachments of ten, fifteen, twenty years to the space. Quite a few of them are reluctant to commit because of the active mobility their work in the cultural field demands, or because of the precarity of their line of work, which cannot ensure continuous money for rent or even staying in such work.

If it isn't long term, what does the future hold for those at SODAS 2123 and in the neighboring area? The most likely scenario is the municipality, after ending the contract, will displace the residents. Organizers will be forced to take their knowledge and skills accrued in this commons elsewhere, which is a painful situation for everyone who put much time and money into remodeling the building. Artist residents disbanding yet again into individual studios here and there in the city—into mostly unsafe environments unusable in East Europe's winters and with far fewer collective and communal ties—has a negative impact on these individual artists, but also the larger self-governing community of artists, and therefore, on the potentialities of wider urban commoning.

The Commonist Horizon

FIGURE 5.3. *People gathered outside Luna6 for "district kitchen" in Summer 2021.*

A horizon has already begun to emerge. From our analysis of the shared conditions of enclaves across the city and a call for the building of thresholds between them so as to *unenclose* the transnational commoner community. Here arises the question of autonomy: how will we gain true autonomy over an infrastructure owned by the municipality and only temporarily leased out for noncommercial use under a capital-directed regeneration policy?

Notably, the autonomy of the commons, as we've already made clear, cannot be based on a simple secession from the state and market—this would only offer a favor to capital, which can now shed the costs of spatial maintenance and social reproduction onto us. The question of autonomy thus becomes a matter of strategic dependency. Framing the difference between an autonomist demand strategy and a reformist one, Neil Gray points to Silvia Federici's considerations of Italy in the 1970s:

As Silvia Federici argued in *Wages Against Housework*, it is one thing to organise communally and then demand that the state pay for it, and another to ask the state to organise communal production: 'In one case we regain some control over our lives, in the other we extend the State's control over us.'[49]

It is from Federici's notion of an autonomist demand that we arrive at our concluding proposal for the constitution of public-common partnerships (PCPs). In what follows we will loosely rehearse a speculative scenario wherein divested agents from enclaves across the city unite in a movement for the constitution of a PCP called the "Naujininkai Commons": a transitory tool on the way to commonism allowing for direct democratic control over the distribution of value, without relying on privatization nor upon the nationalization and centralization of the infrastructures and enterprises seized.

The idea of public-common partnerships was borne out of problems experienced by small-scale enclaves—such as a consumer or housing cooperatives—in the predatory financial marketplace which favors profit over social value. PCPs are also a strategic response to the historical failings of state socialist efforts to take control of social reproduction through nationalization. Through the seizure of private and public infrastructures, PCPs go beyond the binary of market/state: they reject the direct nationalization and municipalization of public resources and services that are held and produced by the communities, as well as the privatization of them (as in the case of public-private partnerships, PPPs). As such, the PCP aims to definancialize public social infrastructures and "sidestep the mechanisms through which finance capital exercises its discipline and structures the economy" by connecting different institutional forms under "common democratic management" so there would be "wider structural changes in our society and economy."[50]

Going into some detail now, in our speculative scenario of a Naujininkai Commons PCP, a popular movement of enclaves would seize the premises of the largest electricity provider in the city, Perlas, which

---

49. Neil Gray, "Whose Rebel City?," *Mute* 3, no. 4 (2012), https://www.metamute.org/editorial/articles/whose-rebel-city.

50. Keir Milburn and Bertie Russell, "Public-Common Partnerships: Building New Circuits of Collective Ownership," *Common Wealth*, June 27, 2019.

was privatized—like all other providers—in the last two years.[51] After its seizure, NC would negotiate an agreement with the municipality, establishing a workers union representing the operators of the enterprise and a commoner association representing member enclaves of NC (i.e., the migrant detention center, Vilnius Social Club, SODAS 2123, Luna6, etc.). The democratically seized enterprise, now absorbed into the NC ecology, is put to use as a semi-autonomous financial tool for not only sustaining the infrastructure but exponentially expanding it—Perlas revenues now being democratically redistributed between the member organizations and municipality.[52] No longer fully dependent on the state for the social redistribution of value, the PCP functions as a transitory mechanism for building the economic autonomy that could enunciate the horizon for a fully commonist transformation of the capitalist political economy.

---

51. In 2020, akin to the European Union laws, electricity provision in Lithuania underwent "demonopolization," which effectively privatized all electricity providers.

52. One notable example is the Cochabamba water company that was commonized following the Bolivian "Water War" in 2000. For more examples of commonized utility companies, see Keir Milburn and Bertie Russell, "Public-Common Partnerships, Autogestion, and the Right to the City," unpublished essay (2021).

BIBLIOGRAPHY

Adorno, Theodor W. *Minima Moralia: Reflections on a Damaged Life*. Translated by E. F. N. Jephcott. London and New York: Verso, 1974.

Aidukaite, Jolanta. "Housing Policy Regime in Lithuania: Towards Liberalization and Marketization." *GeoJournal* 79, no. 4 (2014): 421–432.

Anonymous. "The Killing of the Elephant and Destruction of the Castle." *Anguish Language*, 2015.

Archer, Rory. "'Imaš kuću—vrati stan.' Housing inequalities, socialist morality, and discontent in 1980s Yugoslavia." *Godišnjak za društvenu istoriju [Annual of Social History]* 20, no. 3 (2015): 119–139.

Archer, Rory. "The moral economy of home construction in late socialist Yugoslavia." *History and Anthropology* 29, no. 2 (2018): 141–162.

Architecture, Forensic. "A Memorial in Exile." *Mute* (June 28, 2012). https://www.met-amute.org/community/your-posts/memorial-exile.

Baća, Bojan. "Practice Theory and Postsocialist Civil Society: Toward a New Analytical Framework." *International Political Sociology* 16, no. 1 (March 2022). https://doi.org/10.1093/ips/olab021.

Barbagallo, Camille, and Silvia Federici. "Introduction: Care Work and the Commons." *The Commoner*, no. 15 (Winter 2012): 1–21.

Berlant, Lauren. "The Commons: Infrastructures for Troubling Times." *Environment and Planning D: Society and Space* 34, no. 3 (2016): 393–419.

Berry, Josephine, and Anthony Iles. "The Exploitation of Isolation: Urban Development and the Artist's Studio." In *Radical Housing: Art, Struggle, Care*, edited by Ana Vilenica, 165–186. Amsterdam: Institute of Network Cultures, 2021.

Bibić, Vedrana, Andrea Milat, Srećko Horvat, and Igor Štiks. *The Balkan Forum: Situations, Struggles, Strategies*. Zagreb: Rosa Luxemburg Stiftung, 2014.

Billard, Jillian. "Art & Gentrification: What is 'Artwashing' and What Are Galleries Doing to Resist It?" *Artspace Magazine*, November 30, 2017. https://www.artspace.com/magazine/art_101/in_depth/art-gentrification-what-is-artwashing-and-what-are-galleries-doing-to-resist-it-55124.

Bishop, Claire. *Artificial Hells: Participatory Art and the Politics of Spectatorship*. London and New York: Verso, 2014.

Böröcz, József. "'Eurowhite' Conceit, 'Dirty White' Ressentment: 'Race' in Europe." *Sociological Forum* 36, no. 4 (December 2021): 1116–1134.

Böröcz, József, and Melinda Kovács. Empire's New Clothes: Unveiling EU Enlargement. Central Europe Review e-books, 2001. http://aei.pitt.edu/144/.

Brooke, Mike. "Even Thames Armada and Sheep Couldn't Stop Docklands Invasion of Isle of Dogs." *East London Advertiser*, October 2, 2017.

Bryan-Wilson, Julia. *Art Workers: Radical Practice in the Vietnam War Era*. Berkeley: University of California Press, 2009.

CareNotes Collective, *For Health Autonomy: Horizons of Care Beyond Austerity—Reflections from Greece*. Brooklyn: Common Notions, 2020.

Čivle, Agnese. "The Messenger of Fluxus for the 21st Century. An interview with Artūras Zuokas, the mayor of Vilnius." *Arterritory*, December 23, 2014. https://arterritory.com/ en/ visual_arts/interviews/12301-the_messenger_of_fluxus_for_the_21st_century/.

Claude, Gregor. "Goatherds in Pinstripes." *Mute* 1, no. 23 (March 2002). https://www. metamute.org/editorial/articles/goatherds-pinstripes.

Creaney, Sean, and Roger Hopkins-Burke. "A 'New' Response to Anti-Social Behaviour: Early Reflections on the Anti-Social Behaviour, Crime and Policing Act 2014." *Safer Communities* 13, no. 4 (2015): 161–170.

Čukić, Iva, and Jovana Timotijević, eds. *Spaces of Commoning: Urban Commons in the Ex-YU Region*. Belgrade: Ministry of Space/Institute for Urban Politics, 2020.

Davies, Anthony, and Simon Ford. "Art Capital." *Art Monthly* 213 (February 1998). http://www.artmonthly.co.uk/magazine/site/article/art-capital-by-simon-ford-and-anthony-davies-february-1998.

Davis, Mike. "Planet of the Slums." *New Left Review* 26 (March/April 2004). https:// newleftreview.org/issues/ii26/articles/mike-davis-planet-of-slums.

De Angelis, Massimo. *Omnia Sunt Communia: On the Commons and the Transformation to Postcapitalism*. London: Zed Books, 2017.

Dean, Jodi. *The Communist Horizon*. New York and London: Verso, 2012.

Deleuze, Gilles and Félix Guattari. *Anti-Oedipus: Capitalism and Schizophrenia*, translated by Robert Hurley, Mark Seem, and Helen Lane. New York: Penguin Group, 1977.

Dolenec, Daniela, and Mislav Žitko. "Ostrom and Horvat: Identifying Principles of a Socialist Governmentality." *Grupa 22 Working Paper Series* (July 2013). https://beyondostrom.blog.rosalux.de/files/2013/09/Dolenec-Zitko-Working-Paper-2013-1.pdf.

Dombroski, Kelly, Gradon Diprose, and Irene Boles. "Can the commons be temporary? The role of transitional commoning in post-quake Christchurch." *Local Environment* 24, no. 4 (January 2019): 313–328.

Džokić, Ana, and Marc Neelan. "Walks on the Wild Side." In *Concurrent Urbanities: Designing Infrastructures of Inclusion*, edited by Miodrag Mitrašinovic, 37–60. New York and Milton, Abingdon, Oxon: Routledge, 2016.

Frost, Alex. "Property Guardian." Flat Time House, London, August 2015. http://flat-timeho.org.uk/projects/publications/alex-frost/.

Gagyi, Ágnes, and András Vigvári. "Informal Practices in Housing financialization: The Transformation of an Allotment Garden in Hungary." *Critical Housing Analysis* 5, no. 2 (2018): 46–55.

Glass, Ruth. "Introduction: Aspects of Change." *London: Aspects of Change*, Centre for Urban Studies Report No. 3. London: MacGibbon & Kee, 1964.

Goffey, Andrew. "Guattari and Transversality: Institutions, Analysis and Experimentation." *Radical Philosophy* (January–February 2016): 38–47.

Goldner, Loren. "Fictitious Capital for Beginners: Imperialism, 'Anti-Imperialism,' and the Continuing Relevance of Rosa Luxemburg." *Mute* 2, no. 6 (August 21, 2007). https://www.metamute.org/editorial/articles/fictitious-capital-beginners-imperialism -anti-imperialism-and-continuing-relevance-rosa-luxemburg.

Gordon, Lewis. "Disaster Aesthetics: How COVID-19 Made the World 'Cute.'" *Art Review*, August 12, 2020. https://artreview.com/disaster-aesthetics-how-covid-19-made-the-world-cute/.

Gray, Neil. "Whose Rebel City?" *Mute* 3, no. 4 (2012): 132–145. https://www.metamute.org/editorial/articles/whose-rebel-city.

Guattari, Félix. *Psychoanalysis and Transversality: Texts and Interviews 1955–1971*, translated by Ames Hodges. Los Angeles: Semiotext(e), 2015).

Guattari, Félix. "Transversality." In *Molecular Revolution: Psychiatry and Politics*, translated by Rosemary Sheed. Harmondsworth: Penguin Books, 1984.

Guy, Nicola. "Art in the Interim: How the Issue of the Restitution of Housing in Reunified Berlin Led to an Artistic Reimagining of the City." In *Radical Housing: Art, Struggle, Care*, edited by Ana Vilenica, 152–164. Amsterdam: Institute of Network Cultures, 2021.

Harris, Andrew. "Livingstone versus Serota: The High-rise Battle of Bankside." *The London Journal* 33, no. 3 (2008): 289–299.

Harvey, David. *Rebel Cities: From the Right to the City to the Urban Revolution*. London and New York: Verso, 2019.

Harvey, David. *A Brief History of Neoliberalism*. Oxford: Oxford University Press, 2011.

Harvey, David. "The Right to the City." *New Left Review* 53 (September/October 2008). https://newleftreview.org/issues/ii53/articles/david-harvey-the-right-to-the-city.

Harvey, David. "The 'New' Imperialism: Accumulation by Dispossession." *Socialist Register* 40 (2004). https://socialistregister.com/index.php/srv/article/view/5811/2707.

Harvey, David. "The Art of Rent: Globalization, Monopoly and the Commodification of Culture." *Socialist Register* 38 (2002): 93–102. https://socialistregister.com/ index.php/srv/article/view/5778/2674.

Harvey, David. "The Spatial Fix: Hegel, von Thunen and Marx." *Antipode* 13, no. 3 (1981): 1–12.

Harrison, Nell. "The end of Lietuva cinema, the death of community culture." *The Baltic Times*, August 6, 2005. https://www.baltictimes.com/news/articles/12887/.

Heartfield, James. "Creative London." *Mute* (October 6, 2007). https://www.metamute.org/editorial/articles/creative-london.

Holm, Andrej, and Armin Kuhn. "Squatting And Urban Renewal." In *Squatting in Europe: Radical Spaces, Urban Struggles*, edited by the Squatting Europe Kollective, 161–184. Wivenhoe/New York/Port Watson: Minor Compositions, 2013.

Horvat, Srećko, and Igor Štiks. *Welcome to the Desert of Post-Socialism: Radical Politics After Yugoslavia*. London and New York: Verso, 2015.

Huselj, Alma. *Lost in Transition: The Legacies of Yugoslav Policies on Serbian Roma's Housing Insecurities*. Princeton University Undergraduate Senior Thesis, 2019. http://arks.princeton.edu/ark:/88435/dsp01nk322h182.

Iles, Anthony. "Midnight Notes Digitized." *Memory of the World Library*, 2015, https://www.memoryoftheworld.org/blog/2015/05/27/repertorium_midnight_notes_digitized.

Iles, Anthony. "Of Lammas Land and Olympic Dreams." *Mute* (January 6, 2007). https://www.metamute.org/editorial/articles/lammas-land-and-olympic-dreams.

Iles, Anthony, and Tom Roberts. *All Knees and Elbows of Susceptibility and Refusal:*

Reading History from Below. London and Glasgow: Strickland Distribution, Transmission Gallery, and Mute, 2012.

Iles, Anthony, and Josephine Berry Slater. *No Room to Move: Radical Art and the Regenerate City.* London: Mute, 2010.

Jacobsson, Kerstin, ed. *Urban Grassroots Movements in Central and Eastern Europe.* Surrey: Ashgate, 2015.

Jelinek, Csaba, Judit Bodnár, Márton Czirfusz, and Zoltán Ginelli. *Kritikai Városkutatás.* Budapest: L'Harmattan, 2013.

Jones, Christopher. "Pyramid Dead – The Artangel of History." *Mute* (April 17, 2014). https://www.metamute.org/editorial/articles/pyramid-dead-artangel-history.

Jovanović, Jelica. "Materializing the Self-Management: Tracking the Commons in Yugoslav Housing." In *Housing as Commons: Housing Alternatives as Response to the Current Urban Crisis*, edited by Stavros Stavrides and Penny Travlou, np. London: Bloomsbury, forthcoming.

Juška, Arūnas. "Privatisation of State Security and Policing in Lithuania." *Policing and Society* 19, no. 3 (2009): 226–246.

Juška, Arūnas. "Rural Marginalization, Policing, and Crime in Lithuania." *Police Practice and Research* 7, no. 5 (December 2006): 431–447.

Juška, Arūnas. "The changing character of criminality and policing in post-socialist Lithuania: From fighting organized crime to policing marginal populations?" *Crime, Law & Social Change*, no. 41 (2004): 161–177.

Kelly, Susan. "The Transversal and the Invisible: How do you really make a work of art that is not a work of art?" *transversal texts* (January 2005). https://transversal.at/transversal/0303/kelly/en.

Kirn, Gal. "Forgotten History of the Commons in Socialist Yugoslavia: A Case of Self-Managed Cultural Infrastructure in the Period of 1960s and 1970s." *TKH Journal for Performing Art Theory*, no. 23 (April 2016): 62–70.

Kováts, Eszter. "Black Block East: Right-Wing Anti-Colonialism and Universalising Postcolonialism." *Berliner Gazette*, December 12, 2021, https://projekte.berlinergazette.de/blackboxeast/.

Kunčinas, Domininkas. "Kablys: Alternative Culture by Hook or by Crook." *Lithuanian Music Link* 22 (January–December 2019). https://www.mic.lt/en/discourses/lithuanian-music-link/no22-january-december-2019/domininkas-kuncinas-kablys-alternative-culture-hook-or-crook/.

Lacmanović, Vedrana and Aleksandra Nestorov, *Politika socijalnog stanovanja: Mogućnosti i stvaranje prava za žene koje su preživele nasilje* (Belgrade: Autonomni ženski centar, 2021).

Lancione, Michele, and AbdouMaliq Simone. "Dwelling in Liminalities, Thinking beyond Inhabitation." *Environment and Planning D: Society and Space* 39, no. 6 (December 2021): 969–975.

Ledeneva, Alena. *Russia's Economy of Favors: Blat, Networking and Informal Exchange.* Cambridge: Cambridge University Press, 1998.

Ledeneva, Alena. "Between Gift and Commodity: The Phenomenon of Blat." *The Cambridge Journal of Anthropology* 19, no. 3 (1996/7): 44–66.

Lefebvre, Henri. *The Production of Space*. Translated by Donald Nicholson-Smith. Oxford and Cambridge: Blackwell, 1991.

Lefebvre, Henri. *The Survival of Capitalism: Reproduction of the Relations of Production*. Translated by Frank Bryant. London and New York: Allison & Busby and St Martin's Press, 1976.

Lemos, Gerard. "Forgotten No Longer." *The Guardian*, September 29, 1999. https://www. theguardian.com/society/1999/sep/29/regeneration.guardiansocietysupplement.

Leps, Anu. *A Crime Forecast for Estonia*. Tallinn: The Estonian State Police, 1994.

Lieven, Anatol. *The Baltic Revolution: Estonia, Latvia, Lithuania and the Path to Independence*. New Haven: Yale University Press, 1994.

Linebaugh, Peter. "Charters of Liberty in Black Face and White Face: Race, Slavery and the Commons." *Mute* 2, no. 2 (November 23, 2005). https://www.metamute.org/ editorial/ articles/charters-liberty-black-face-and-white-face-race-slavery-and-commons

Linebaugh, Peter. *Stop, Thief! The Commons, Enclosures, and Resistance*. Oakland: PM Press, 2014.

Lovink, Geert. "Interview with Nomeda & Gediminas. Hacking Public Spaces in Vilnius: Politics of a new media space inside the Lietuva (soviet) cinema." June 20, 2005. https://networkcultures.org/geertlovink-archive/interviews/ interview-with-nomeda-gediminas/.

Lyubchenko, Oleana. "On the Frontier of Whiteness? Expropriation, War, and Social Reproduction in Ukraine." *LeftEast*, April 30, 2022. https://lefteast.org/ frontiers-of-whiteness-expropriation-war-social-reproduction-in-ukraine/.

Marvin, Simon, and Steve Graham. *Splintering Urbanism: Networked Infrastructures, Technological Mobilities and the Urban Condition*. Oxford: Routledge, 2001.

Marx, Karl. *Capital, Vol. 1: A Critique of Political Economy*. Translated by Samuel Moore and Edward Aveling (New York: Modern Library, 1906).

Marx, Karl. *Grundrisse: Foundations of the Critique of Political Economy*. Translated by Martin Nicolaus. New York: Vintage, 1973.

Mayer, Margit, Catharina Thörn, and Håkan Thörn, eds. *Urban Uprisings: Challenging Neoliberal Urbanism in Europe*. London: Springer, 2016.

Michelkevičė, Lina. "*Tarp meno ir politikos. Pro-testo laboratorija kaip viešosios erdvės steigtis* [Between Art and Politics: Pro-test Laboratory as Establishment of Public Space]." Goethe-Institut Litauen, April 2013. https://www.goethe.de/ins/lt/lt/kul/ mag/20550207.html.

Milburn, Keir, and Bertie Russell. "Public-Common Partnerships Building New Circuits of Collective Ownership." *Common Wealth*, June, 27, 2019. https:// www.common-wealth.co.uk/reports/public-common-partnerships-building-new-circuits-of-collective-ownership.

Milburn, Keir, and Bertie Russell. "Public-Common Partnerships, Autogestion, and the Right to the City." Unpublished, 2021.

Minton, Anna. "What Kind of World are We Building? The Privatisation of Public Space." RICS, 2006. https://www.annaminton.com/single-post/2016/05/03/ what-kind-of-world-are-we-building-the-privatization-of-public-space.

Moreno, Louis. "The Urban Process under Financialized Capitalism." *City* 18, no. 3

(June 2014): 244–268.

Pajvančić-Cizelj, Ana, and Marina Hjuson. "Urbanization and Urban Planning at the European Semi-Periphery: Unintended Gender Consequences." *Sociologija* 60, no. 1 (2018): 275–287.

Pasquinelli, Matteo. *Animal Spirits: A Bestiary of the Commons*. Rotterdam and Amsterdam: NAi and Institute of Network Cultures, 2008.

Perlman, Fredy. "The Continuing Appeal of Nationalism." *Fifth Estate* (Winter 1984), https://theanarchistlibrary.org/library/fredy-perlman-the-continuing-appeal-of-nationalism.

Pilditch, David. "£400m cuts leave museums in crisis," *Express*, January 29, 2019, https://www.express.co.uk/news/uk/1079497/400m-cuts-museums-crisis-libraries-public-fundings.

Pogány, István. "Pariah Peoples: Roma and the Multiple Failures of Law in Central and Eastern Europe." *Social & Legal Studies* 21, no. 3 (2012): 375–393.

Porcupine, Peter. "Footnote: Defending the Commons." *Here and Now* 14 (1993): 60–61. https://libcom.org/article/here-and-now-14.

Roberts, Peter. "Table of the Evolution of Urban Regeneration." In *Urban Regeneration: A Handbook*, edited by Peter Roberts and Hugh Sykes. London, Thousand Oaks, New Delhi: Sage, 2000.

Roberts, Peter, and Hugh Sykes, eds. *Urban Regeneration: A Handbook*. London, Thousand Oaks, New Delhi: Sage, 2000.

Romer, Christy. "Artist squares up to Regulator over 'manifestly unreasonable' fundraising investigation." *Arts Professional*, June 28, 2017. https://www.artsprofessional.co.uk/ news/exclusive-artist-squares-regulator-over-manifestly-unreasonable-fundraising-investigation.

Rudnicki, Cezary. "An Ethics for Stateless Socialism: An Introduction to Edward Abramowski's Political Philosophy." *Praktyka Teoretyczna* 1, no. 27 (2018): 20–33.

Saler, Michael T. *The Avant-Garde in Interwar England: Medieval Modernism and the London Underground*. New York and Oxford: Oxford University Press, 2001.

Šarūnas, Tadas. "The Pleasures and Pains of a Changing City." Presentation [on gentrification in the Vilnius Train Station District,] facilitated by Naujininkai Commons, Luna6, Vilnius, November 10, 2021.

Seymour, Benedict. "Drowning by Numbers: The Non-Reproduction of New Orleans." *Mute*, December 21, 2006. https://www.metamute.org/editorial/articles/drowning-numbers-non-reproduction-new-orleans.

Slavka, Zeković, Ksenija Petovar, and Bin Md Saman Nor-Hisham. "The Credibility of Illegal and Informal Construction: Assessing Legalization Policies in Serbia," *Cities* 97 (February 2020): 1–12. https://doi.org/10.1016/j.cities.2019.102548.

Smith, Neil. *The New Urban Frontier: Gentrification and the Revanchist City*. London: Routledge, 1996.

Smith, Neil. "Toward a Theory of Gentrification: A Back to the City Movement by Capital, not People." *Journal of the American Planning Association* 45, no. 4 (1979): 538–548.

Sosunova, Anastasia. *Express Method*. Vilnius: Swallow Gallery, 2021.

Stavrides, Stavros. *Common Space: The City as Commons*. London: Zed Books, 2018.

Stoll, Tamara. *Ridley Road Market*. Self-published, London, 2019.

Standl, Harald, and Dovilė Krupickaitė, "Gentrification in Vilnius (Lithuania): The Example of Užupis." *Europa Regional* 12, no. 1 (2004): 42–51.

Swyngedouw, Erik. "Apocalypse Now! Fear and Doomsday Pleasure." *Capitalism Nature Socialism* 24, no. 1 (2013): 9–18.

Thieme, Tatiana A. "Beyond Repair: Staying with Breakdown at the Interstices." *Environment and Planning: Society and Space* 39, no. 6 (July 2021): 1092–1110.

Tomašević, Tomislav, Vedran Horvat, Alma Midžić, Ivana Dragšić, and Miodrag Dakić. *Commons in South East Europe: Case of Croatia, Bosnia & Herzegovina and Macedonia*. Zagreb: Institute for Political Ecology, 2018.

Tomba, Massimiliano. *Marx's Temporalities [Historical Materialism* 44]. Leiden: Koninklijke Brill NV, 2013.

Tomba, Massimiliano. *Insurgent Universality: An Alternative Legacy of Modernity*. New York: Oxford University Press, 2019.

Trilupaitytė, Skaidra. "Artistic Protest and (Political) Critique: Vilnius Examples of the First Decade of the XXI Century." *Art History & Criticism* 11 (2015): 5–21.

Tsing, Anna. *The Mushroom at the End of the World*. Princeton, NJ: Princeton University Press, 2015.

Vilenica, Ana. "Contradictions and Antagonisms in (Anti-) Social(ist) Housing in Serbia." *ACME: An International Journal for Critical Geographies* 18, no. 6 (December 2019): 1261–1282.

Vilenica, Ana. "The Doomed Pursuit of Dignity: Artists as Property Guardians in and Against Artwashing." *AM Journal*, no. 25 (2021). https://fmkjournals.fmk.edu.rs/index.php/AM/ article/view/455/Vilenica_AM25.

Vilenica, Ana and Pražić, Ivana. "Why All of 'Us' Are Challenged to Struggle against 'Whiteness,'" *Berliner Gazette*, December 13, 2021. https://blogs.mediapart.fr/berliner-gazette/blog/131221/black-box-east-why-all-us-are-challenged-struggle-against-whiteness.

Vilenica, Ana, Vladimir Mentus, Irena Ristić. "Struggles for Care Infrastructures in Serbia: The Pandemic, Dispossessed Care, and Housing." *Historical Social Research* 46, no. 4 (December 2021): 189–208.

Vilenica, Ana, Ana Džokic, and Marc Neelen. "Affordable housing in your lifetime?" In *The Social Production of Architecture—Politics, Values and Actions in Contemporary Practice*, edited by Doina Petrescu and Kim Trogal, 245–257. London: Routledge, 2017.

Vishmidt, Marina. "All Shall Be Unicorns: About Commons, Aesthetics and Time." *Open!* (September 2014). https://onlineopen.org/all-shall-be-unicorns.

Vishmidt, Marina. "Mimesis of the Hardened and Alienated: Social Practice as Business Model." *e-flux journal*, no. 43 (March 2013). https://www.e-flux.com/journal/43/60197/mimesis-of-the-hardened-and-alienated-social-practice-as-business-model/.

Vuksanović-Macura, Zlata. "Spatial Segregation of Roma Settlements within Serbian Cities. Examples from Belgrade, Novi Sad, and Kruševac." In *Spatial Conflicts and*

Divisions in Post-socialist Cities, edited by Valentin Mihaylov, 211–224. New York: Springer, 2020.

Waliuzzaman, S M. *A Commons Perspective on Urban Informal Settlements: A Study of Kalyanpur slum in Dhaka, Bangladesh*. PhD dissertation. School of Earth and Environment, University of Canterbury, Auckland, New Zealand (October 2020).

Windsor, Joshua. "Desire Lines: Deleuze and Guattari on Molar Lines, Molecular Lines, and Lines of Flight." *New Zealand Sociology* 30, no. 1 (2015): 156–170.

Zeković, Slavka, Tamara Maričić, and Marija Cvetinović. "Transformation of Housing Policy in a Post-Socialist City: The Example of Belgrade." *Regulating the City: Contemporary Urban Housing Law*, edited by Julian Sidoli, Marvin Noah Frank Kiehl, and Michel Vols, 41–64. The Hague: Eleven International Publishing, 2017.

Zibechi, Raúl. *Territories in Resistance: A Cartography of Latin American Social Movements*. Oakland: AK Press, 2012.

Zukin, Sharon. *Loft Living: Culture and Capital in Urban Change*. Baltimore and London: The Johns Hopkins University Press, 1982.

ABOUT THE EDITORS

Mary N. Taylor is a militant researcher living in New York City whose praxis sits at the intersection of anthropology, dialogical art, and urbanism. She studies social movements, urbanization, solidarity, and the body. She has taught and learned in many places and strives towards revolutionary processes of knowledge production. She is a founding member of the *LeftEast* collective and Know Waste Lands Garden.

Noah Brehmer is a militant researcher, editor, and union member, who moved from NYC to Vilnius, Lithuania in 2013. In Vilnius, he organizes through movement space Luna6. In 2022, Brehmer cofounded Lost Property Press with Vaida Stepanovaitė. Brehmer has published articles and essays in *Blind Field Journal, LeftEast, Mute, Metropolis M, Artnews.lt,* and *OpenDemocracy.*

ABOUT THE CONTRIBUTORS

The Naujininkai Commons Collective was formed in 2021 to confront the regeneration project "Vilnius Connect." Exploring the urban commons as an alternative to capital-led urban development, the collective seeks to foster community centered standpoints for the district's future. Naujininkai Commons operates as a militant research group, educational platform, and anti-regeneration organizing initiative. Over the last year the collective has organized a series of collective readings, actions, workshops, discussions, and District Kitchen events, in hopes to not only participate in district level commoning, but to also join a trans-local conversation where experiences may be critically compared and broader movement strategies propagated as a common, international, horizon. While the collective has been shaped by numerous contributors the chapter for this book was produced by three members: **Vaiva Aglinskas** is a PhD candidate in Cultural Anthropology at CUNY Graduate Center, whose research focuses on the spatial and social costs of urban development projects in Vilnius; **Noah Brehmer** is a founding member of Luna6; **Vaida Stepanovaitė** is a PhD candidate in Visual

Cultures at Goldsmiths College, conducting practice-based research on the tensions between the institutive, the radical, and the communal in the contemporary art field.

Ana Vilenica is a Postdoctoral Research Fellow for the European Research Council (ERC) project "Inhabiting Radical Housing" at the Polytechnic and University of Turin's Inter-university Department of Regional & Urban Studies and Planning (DIST). She is editor of *Radical Housing Journal*, Central and East Europe editor at *Interface: Journal for and about Social Movements*, and the editor of five books, most recently *Radical Housing: Art, Struggle, Care* (2021). She is a long-term housing, feminist, and no-borders activist in Serbia and the UK who writes about housing struggles, migrant struggles, feminist struggles, antiracism struggles, social movements, and engaged art practices. Ana is a recipient of the Marie Skłodowska-Curie Individual Fellowship for her project focusing on housing deprivation and citizen initiatives in Serbia and the UK. She is currently developing a new agenda for research on transnational organizing within and beyond radical housing struggles.

Anthony Iles is a founding member of Full Unemployment Cinema, an editor with *Mute/Metamute* (2005–2022) and coauthor, with Josephine Berry, of *No Room to Move: Art and the Regenerate City* (2011) and with Tom Roberts, of *All Knees and Elbows of Susceptibility and Refusal: Reading History from Below* (2012). He is commissioning editor of *Anguish Language: Writing and Crisis* (2015), *Look at Hazards, Look at Losses* (2017) and a contributor to *Brave New Work: A Reader on Harun Farocki's Film* A New Product (2014) and the *ULWC Reader* (2021). Essays and reviews by Anthony have been published in *Variant, Cesura//Acceso, Mute, Radical Philosophy, Rab-Rab: Journal for Political and Formal Inquiries in Art*, and *Logos*.

Zsuzsanna Pósfai is a founding member of Periféria Policy and Research Center, an independent organization focusing on issues of urban development and spatial and housing justice. She holds an MA in Urban and Regional Policy from Sciences Po Paris and wrote her PhD (University of Szeged) about the spatial aspects of housing finance. Her research focuses on the financialization of housing and the indebtedness of households. She is active—both professionally and practically—in establishing a model for rental-based housing cooperatives in Hungary.

Ágnes Gagyi works on East European politics and social movements in the context of the region's long-term world economic and geopolitical integration. Her current research at the University of Gothenburg looks at the social conditions of urban green infrastructures in face of the climate crisis. She is a member of Solidarity Economy Center (Budapest), an organization facilitating solidarity economy ecosystems.

CareNotes Collective is a militant research project organizing around the centrality of care in movements against capitalist and state domination. The global intensification of inequality and violence have heightened the need to deepen our capacity to resist, offer concrete alternatives, and reproduce ourselves in the process. CareNotes Collective seeks to record and amplify the experiences of those struggling for health autonomy in their own communities. Its central challenge is to imagine how to expand these practices while defending our communities from cooption, state violence, emotional as well as financial domination, and trauma.

ABOUT COMMON NOTIONS

Common Notions is a publishing house and programming platform that fosters new formulations of living autonomy. We aim to circulate timely reflections, clear critiques, and inspiring strategies that amplify movements for social justice.

Our publications trace a constellation of critical and visionary meditations on the organization of freedom. By any media necessary, we seek to nourish the imagination and generalize common notions about the creation of other worlds beyond state and capital. Inspired by various traditions of autonomism and liberation—in the US and internationally, historical and emerging from contemporary movements—our publications provide resources for a collective reading of struggles past, present, and to come.

Common Notions regularly collaborates with political collectives, militant authors, radical presses, and maverick designers around the world. Our political and aesthetic pursuits are dreamed and realized with Antumbra Designs.

www.commonnotions.org
info@commonnotions.org

ABOUT LOST PROPERTY PRESS

Lost Property Press (LPP) is a publishing platform with a communal itch. Operating from Vilnius, Lithuania, LPP is committed to cultivating shared notions and strategies between movements in the post-state socialist East and beyond. More than producing books—the reification of social knowledge as property—LPP is about durational, paracademic, mutinous publishing processes.

Also available from Lost Property Press:

Paths to Autonomy, edited by Noah Brehmer and Vaida Stepanovaitė (copublished with Minor Compositions / Autonomedia)

**LOST
PROPERTY
PRESS**

BECOME A COMMON NOTIONS MONTHLY SUSTAINER

These are decisive times ripe with challenges and possibility, heartache, and beautiful inspiration. More than ever, we need timely reflections, clear critiques, and inspiring strategies that can help movements for social justice grow and transform society.

Help us amplify those words, deeds, and dreams that our liberation movements, and our worlds, so urgently need.

Movements are sustained by people like you, whose fugitive words, deeds, and dreams bend against the world of domination and exploitation.

For collective imagination, dedicated practices of love and study, and organized acts of freedom.

By any media necessary.
With your love and support.

Monthly sustainers start at $12 and $25.

commonnotions.org/sustain

*The Feminist Subversion of the Economy:
Contributions to Life Against Capital*
Amaia Pérez Orozco
Translated by Liz Mason-Deese

978-1-942173-19-9
$22.00
288 pages

In the face of unending economic crises and climate catastrophe, we must consider, what does a dignified life look like? Feminist intellectual and activist Amaia Pérez Orozco powerfully and provocatively outlines a vision for a web of life sustained collectively with care, mutualism, and in balance with our ecological world. That vision is a call to action to subvert the foundational order of racial capitalism, colonial violence, and a heteropatriarchal economy that threatens every form of life.

The Feminist Subversion of the Economy makes the connection between the systems that promise more devastation and destruction of life in the name of profit—and rallies women, LGBTQ+ communities, and movements worldwide to center gender and social reproduction in a vision for a balanced ecology, a just economy, and a free society.

MORE FROM COMMON NOTIONS

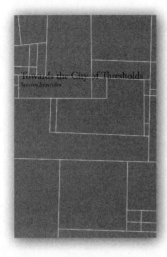

Towards the City of Thresholds
Stavros Stavrides

978-1-942173-09-0
$20.00
272 pages

Towards the City of Thresholds is a pioneering and ingenious study of these new forms of socialization and uses of space—self-managed and communal—that passionately reveals cities as the sites of manifest social antagonism as well as spatialities of emancipation. Activist and architect Stavros Stavrides describes the powerful reinvention of politics and social relations stirring everywhere in our urban world and analyzes the theoretical underpinnings present in these metropolitan spaces and how they might be bridged to expand the commons.

What is the emancipatory potential of the city in a time of crisis? What thresholds must be crossed for us to realize this potential? To answer these questions, Stavrides draws penetrating insight from the critical philosophies of Walter Benjamin, Michel Foucault, and Henri Lefebvre—among others—to challenge the despotism of the political and urban crises of our times and reveal the heterotopias immanent within them.

MORE FROM COMMON NOTIONS

19 and 20: Notes For a New Insurrection
Colectivo Situaciones
With Marcello Tarì, Liz Mason-Deese,
Antonio Negri, and Michael Hardt

978-1-942173-48-9
$20.00
288 pages

19 and 20 tells the story of one of the most popular uprising against neo-liberalism: on December 19th and 20th, 2001, amidst a financial crisis that tanked the economy, ordinary people in Argentina took to the streets shouting "¡Qué se vayan todos!" (They all must go!) Thousands of people went to their windows banging pots and pans, neighbors organized themselves into hundreds of popular assemblies, workers took over streets and factories. In those exhilarating days, government after government fell as people invented a new economy and a new way of governing themselves.

It was a defining moment of the antiglobalization movement and Colectivo Situaciones was there, thinking and engaging in the struggle. Today, as a staggering debt crisis deepens amidst an already COVID-shaken economy, we see the embers from that time twenty years ago in the mutual aid initiatives and new forms of solidarity amidst widespread vulnerability.

Revisiting the forms of counterpower that emerged from the shadow of neoliberal rule, Colectivo Situaciones reminds us that our potential is collective and ungovernable.

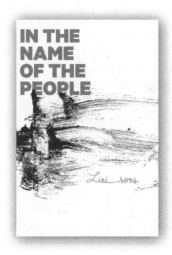

In the Name of the People
Liaisons

978-1-942173-07-6
$18.00
208 pages

In the Name of the People is an analysis and reflection on the global populist surge, written from the local forms it takes in the places we inhabit: the United States, Catalonia, France, Italy, Japan, Korea, Lebanon, Mexico, Quebec, Russia, and Ukraine. The upheaval and polarizations caused by populist policies around the world indicates above all the urgency to develop a series of planetary revolutionary interpretations, and to make the necessary connections in order to understand and act in the world.

The ghost of the People has returned to the world stage, claiming to be the only force capable of correcting or taking charge of the excesses of the time. This truly internationalist and collectivist publication boldly examines the forms of right and leftwing populism emergent in the fissures of the political world. Experimental in both form and analysis, *In the Name of the People* is the commune form of thought and text.

For Health Autonomy:
Horizons of Care Beyond Austerity—
Reflections from Greece
CareNotes Collective

978-1-942173-14-4
$15
144 Pages

The present way of life is a war against our bodies. Nearly everywhere, we are caught in a crumbling health system that furthers our misery and subordination to the structural violence of capital and a state that only intensifies our general precarity. Can we build the capacity and necessary infrastructure to heal ourselves and transform the societal conditions that continue to mentally and physically harm us?

Amidst the perpetual crises of capitalism is a careful resistance—organized by medical professionals and community members, students and workers, citizens and migrants. These projects operate in fierce resistance to austerity, state violence and abandonment, and the neoliberal structure of the healthcare industry that are failing people.

For Health Autonomy is a powerful collection of first-hand accounts of those who join together to build new possibilities of care and develop concrete alternatives based on the collective ability of communities and care workers to replace our dependency on police and prisons.